John B.
KEANE

Sharon's
Grave

MERCIER PRESS
Cork
www.mercierpress.ie

First published in 1961 by Progress House (Publications) Ltd.
This edition 2015

© John B. Keane 1960,1967, 1975, 1995

ISBN: 978 1 89817 502 5

Printed and bound in the EU.

To Michael Ó h-Aodha

Sharon's Grave was first produced at the Father Mathew Hall, Cork, on 1 February 1960, by the Southern Theatre Group, with the following cast

Donal Conlee	CHARLES GINNANE
Peadar Minogue	SEAMUS MOYNIHAN
Trassie Conlee	MAURA HASSETT
Neelus Conlee	MICHAEL TWOMEY
Dinzie Conlee	EAMON KEANE
Jack Conlee	FLOR DULLEA
Mague	MARIE TWOMEY
Moll	MAIRE MCLOUGHLIN
Tom Shaun	TOM VESEY
Miss Dee	KAY HEALY
Pats Bo Bwee	JAMES N. HEALY

The play was produced by Dan Donovan, with settings by Frank Sanquest.

This new version of *Sharon's Grave* was first presented by The Gate Theatre on 25 July 1995 with the following cast:

Donal Conlee	CECIL BELL
Peadar Minogue	STEPHEN HOGAN
Trassie Conlee	CATHERINE BYRNE
Neelus Conlee	BRIAN O'BYRNE
Dinzie Conlee	MARK O'REGAN
Jack Conlee	PAT KINEVANE
Miss Dee	CAROLINE GRAY
Pats Bo Bwee	JOHN OLOHAN
Chorus	ELIZABETH BRACKEN
	OLIVIA CAFFREY
	AMELIA CROWLEY
	EILEEN MCCLOSKEY
	JENNIFER O'DEA

The play was produced by Ben Barnes, with settings by Frank Conway, costume design by Jo Taylor and lightning by Tina MacHugh

ACT ONE
SCENE ONE

The action takes place in a bedroom in a small farmhouse on an isolated headland on the south-western seaboard of Ireland.

From the window, and through the open door, can be seen a dreary stretch of mountain, falling down to the sea. Crooked thorn-trees are everywhere along the mountainside and distant crags are evident also.

The room is poorly furnished. A large iron bed. An old iron washstand, in which a basin and ewer are deposited. A small wooden table, and hanging over the bed a large St Brigid's Cross.

An old man, emaciated, with white, scant hair, sits, propped by pillows, on the bed. He faces the audience. A bright quilt covers his lower body. In his hands a rosary beads rests. He would appear to be asleep.

The time is a late evening in March-ending, the year 1925. A knock is heard at the front door.

The man on the bed inclines his body barely, but does not otherwise heed the knock. The knock occurs secondly. A little louder. No movement from the old man on the bed. The latch on the door lifts and the door opens. Enter Peadar Minogue. He is a well-made man, 35 or so, with a weather-beaten copper-coloured face. He wears an old felt hat on his head, an old three-quarter length leather jacket and strong boots. His trouser-ends are tucked inside his rough socks. He carries a large satchel on his back.

For a while he looks at the form on the bed, and then peers closely at the old man ...

Peadar: (*Tentatively*) In pardon to you, sir. Could I disturb you?

(*The old man does not move*)

If you're asleep, sir, I won't wake you. Maybe you're only dozing and you might hear me. I'm looking for directions. (Looks around room) Maybe I'm in the right house, but I don't know. (Doubtfully, to himself) I shouldn't be here if 'tis the wrong house, disturbing people in their privacy, stealing into a place and witnessing things not meant for me. (*Then, kindly, to the old man*) Sleep your good sleep, old man.

(*The old man stirs but barely, and inclines his head to Peadar, who bends near him. The old man moans a little, tries to convey something, fails, and is still again*)

Would you be sick now, by any chance, and not be able to dress your thoughts in words? I don't know! (*Turns and surveys the room again*) If you're sick, there will be somebody attending to you before we're older. I hope it isn't sick you are but asleep. I hope somebody comes in. I'll bide my time. They'll hardly turn me away. (*Takes off his satchel, places it on the floor, tiptoes to the window, peers out*) No sign of a being or animal to be seen!

(*Peadar turns from the window, goes to the door, opens it and looks out, and stands a while in thought, looking into the distance. As he stands thus, a woman enters, silently, from the left. She is dressed in a dark frock, covered by a sacking apron, and wears strong boots. A cloth is tied tightly about her hair. She carries a bunch of daffodils in one hand and a short-stemmed earthenware vase in the other. She is slightly startled and looks in perplexity at Peadar, who does not see her. She makes a sound and Peadar wheels suddenly and looks at her, sweeping off his hat and clutching it in his hands. The woman is Trassie Conlee, thirtyish, of good carriage)*

Trassie: Who are you?

Peadar: My name is Peadar Minogue.

Trassie: Peadar Minogue! There are no Minogues in these parts.

Peadar: I am not from these parts. Is this the townland of Baltavinn?

Trassie: It is!

Peadar: Would this, by any chance, be the house of Donal Conlee?

Trassie: It is. That's Donal Conlee there in the bed.

Peadar: (*Looks at Donal*) It's a strange thing to see a door leading into a bedroom, a door any man might walk in from the road.

Trassie: There were two holdings here in time gone. There are two doors still. We often thought to close one.

Peadar: Who are you?

Trassie: I am Trassie Conlee, his daughter (*Indicating bed*). He isn't well.

Peadar: I thought he might be sick.

Trassie: Would you sit down?

Peadar: Thanks, I will. (*Closes door*) There is a fall of ground the whole way from here to the sea, I saw from the door. A healthy place and a wholesome place to live in. There is no air like the sea air.

Trassie: You can hear the sea here all of the time while there is quietness; at night above all. The sea is all around you. We live on a headland here.

Peadar: I saw that from the rise of ground. Not many houses hereabouts?

(Peadar circles and sits on a chair at the left of the bed. Trassie places flowers in a vase and places the vase on a table)

Trassie: (*Notices satchel*) Did you come far today?

Peadar: From Carraig Head.

Trassie: A good journey. You must have business in these parts?

Peadar: I'm a journeyman thatcher. I heard there were houses in the townland of Baltavinn that needed thatching.

Trassie: It's early in the year now for thatching.

Peadar: Work is hard to come by. No harm to try here for it. I saw the thatch of this house from the road. 'Tis rotting in every quarter. I heard in the next townland – Roseerin, I think they call it – that I would find a few day's work in the house of Donal Conlee. They never said a word about there being sickness in the house.

Trassie: They'll never say that! 'Twas a pity you came so far with a false account. Anyway, while you're here, you'll drink tea.

Peadar: No ... No ... Don't bother yourself ... you have enough to think of ...

Trassie: I would be making it, anyway. I have a brother – Neelus; he is carting seaweed with the pony.

Peadar: It's good to have somebody in the house with you, especially with sickness.

Trassie: Did they tell you in Roseerin about him?

Peadar: Your brother?

Trassie: Yes, my brother.

Peadar: No word of him. His name was not drawn down one way or the other.

Trassie: Did they say anything about me?

Peadar: No! (*Significantly*) Only that the house of Donal Conlee would fall if it wasn't thatched.

Trassie: (*Smiling*) Looking for custom are you?

Peadar: Only what they said. (*Smiles*) A man in search of work will go all roads to come by it.

Trassie: What did they say about my brother Neelus?

Peadar: (*Smiles faintly*) There was no mention of him. Why do you ask the second time?

Trassie: (*Re-arranging the clothes on the bed, hesitantly*) Neelus is strange. He is a good worker – a great worker, but he is a small bit strange. People here in Baltavinn are saying he thinks of nothing but women, day in, day out; nothing but women! They do not know he is kind and gentle and they do not know he will wash the ware for me after the meals and make the beds. All they say is that he is mad for women! Which is a lie for them.

Peadar: Are there no women in Baltavinn?

Trassie: (*Surprised*) There are no girls here, only myself.

Peadar: Are there many men?

Trassie: Only a few, but all would marry if they could. There are no women of my age here. The famine swept most of 'em years ago and the ships took the rest.

Peadar: (*Indicating the old man*) What sickness has he?

Trassie: The heart! Three different attacks he has put over him. He was anointed yesterday by the priest. The doctor said there was only a little life left in him.

Peadar: What did the priest say?

Trassie: That he was not long for this world – to expect it any minute.

Peadar: The tag of death is on all of us. (*Sympathetically*) He looks to be a good age. A life lived out is no loss much.

Trassie: No loss to you.

Peadar: True. (*There is silence between them*)

Trassie: Is there anything else you do but thatch?

Peadar: I will do any work that will give me a good diet, a fire to warm by, and a bed to sleep in.

Trassie: Are you a married man?

Peadar: No! Travelling from one parish to another – no woman wants a man who won't sit still.

Trassie: (*Listening attitude*) That's Neelus putting the pony in.

(*Peadar rises*)

Trassie: Stay sitting, let you. There is no harm in him only foolishness. Stay sitting and don't be put astray by what he tells you. I'll put your bag out of the way.

(*Trassie takes the bag and exits left with it. Peadar surveys the man*) *in the bed, rises, and looks out the window curi-ously. Enter Trassie)*

Trassie: Why are you looking out?

Peadar: No harm intended ... (*Doubtfully*) If I should go, tell me!

Trassie: Wait and have tea. Sit down, or he will be asking questions about you. Surely you will have a mouthful of tea and a forkful of meat cold before you go. (Suggestive) Or maybe 'tis how you're afraid of things you do not meet every day.

Peadar: I'm not afraid, but I would hate to be the cause of upsetting the house by staying a while.

Trassie: There is no fear you will do that, but a sweet plate of bacon would give you heart for your journey.

Peadar: You make me feel hungry. (*Pause*) Does he know his father is bad?

Trassie: In his own way. A different way from ours, but he knows. He knows something is wrong. He is worried from that.

Peadar: (*Nods his head understanding*) Did he ever give you trouble?

Trassie: Not him! He is always helpful. Anything I tell him do, he will do. (*Worried*) Not him, but others are always making trouble.

(Peadar looks at her for a spell and returns to his chair)

Trassie: (*Change of tone*) Of a Sunday Neelus will go down to Carraig Head and go in hiding about the cliffs. He will spend his day watching the sea. If the sea is wild and making noise, he will come home deaf and you might as well be idle as to try and talk to him. If the sea is resting, he will come home saying things to himself ... strange things. (*Awkwardly*) He talks of the wind and the sea and Sharon's grave ...

Peadar: (*Solemnly*) Some men are like that from thinking too much about women.

(*Peadar stirs nervously in his chair. Enter Neelus Conlee from the left. He is twentyish, dressed in tattered smock and waders. He has a vacant look, yet is handsome and refined of face. He looks puzzled when he sees Peadar*)

Trassie: This is Peadar Minogue, Neelus. He was passing the road and he called, asking the way ...

Neelus: (*Smiling*) Peadar Minogue ... Trassie ...

(*Trassie looks hopefully at Peadar*)

Peadar: Very happy to meet you.

Neelus: (*Shakes hands with Peadar*) Pleased the same.

Peadar: (*Tentatively*) I heard good things about you.

Neelus: (*Suspicious*) Where did you hear them?

Peadar: Oh, lots of places ... Glounsharoon and Coilbwee and Kilbaha. Everywhere you could imagine.

13

Neelus: (*Hurtfully*) What used they be saying about me?

Peadar: Oh, you know the way people do be?

Neelus: Used they be telling you about me and the women? (*Peadar looks doubtfully at Trassie*)

Trassie: I'll lay the table for the tea. (*Moves towards the left, then loudly to Neelus*) If he wakes, call me.

(*Exit Trassie. Neelus moves closer to Peadar*)

Neelus: Go on about the women.

Peadar: (*Doubtfully, delicately*) They were saying you were a gifted hand with the ladies.

Neelus: Were they telling you about me and Sharon with her golden hair? (Cautiously) And Shíofra, the little vixen, with her face like the storm?

Peadar: (*Thoughtfully, weighing up Neelus*) It seems to come to me that I heard talks of you and these women you mention. (Sureness) Yes, I heard tell of it in several places. Yes, I'm sure now I did.

Neelus: They don't believe it, you know – a lot of them. They do be laughing at me, especially the girls in the mainland when we go to the chapel on a Sunday. I've seen them pointing me out (*Cautiously*) and I've heard giggling and whispering. Sharon has beautiful hair, red and golden like the sunset (*Elaborates with his hands*) shining like the summer sea and her skin as white as new milk and her voice is rich and deep and sweeter than the voice of a thrush. You never saw her golden hair?

Peadar: No, I never saw her golden hair but I have heard of it. Of course I know the way a girl's hair is and I can imagine what Sharon's would be like.

Neelus: (*Shrewdly*) What did you hear about it?

Peadar: I have forgotten most of it but I remember to hear it was brighter than gold.

(*Neelus studies him suspiciously, and is then apparently satisfied*)

Neelus: Shíofra is a little demon.

Peadar: Shíofra?

Neelus: Did you see Sharon's grave when you were coming here?

Peadar: No.

Neelus: (*Looks about cautiously and confides to Peadar*) Did you not hear of it?

Peadar: (*Interested*) What about it?

Neelus: (*Withdrawing a little – astonished*) You never heard tell of Sharon's grave?

(*There is a distant look about him and awe in his voice*)

It's a great deep hole over there on the cliffs. There is

no bottom to it. It sinks down into the middle of the earth and water is always wild and wilful in it, , even when the rest of the sea is calm.

Peadar: Why is it called Sharon's grave?

Neelus: (*Suddenly brought back to reality, eager to relate his obsession*) Sharon was a young princess of ancient times. Her father was a powerful chieftain in the county of Tyrconnell in the North country. Sharon was gentler than a doe and sweeter than wild honey. Her wild hair fell down over her white shoulders like a golden cape. (*Looks out the window, a sad note in his voic*e) Sharon was travelling on horseback to the rich country of the Maharees down the coast. She was being married to a handsome chieftain with far lands and a tall castle rising over the sea ... (*He pauses*)

Peadar: Go on! What's the rest of the story?

Neelus: Shíofra was the name of Sharon's handmaiden. She was swarthy and humped and ugly and jealous of Sharon because Sharon was so beautiful. She poisoned the warriors of Sharon's father and there was no one left to help poor Sharon (*Reflective sadness*), poor beautiful Sharon, and the old people say that Shíofra whispered a spell in the horse's ear when they were passing the great hole down below and the animal reared and jumped into the hole with Sharon upon its back ...

Peadar: Shíofra was an evil creature! Did she wed the young chieftain herself?

Neelus: Oh, no, indeed! (Shakes his head) No – no, indeed, she did not, for, as the horse was about to fall into the hole, Sharon made one last attempt to save herself and her fingers seized on Shíofra's girdle and she carried the wicked woman with her.

Peadar: And that is why they call it Sharon's grave?

Neelus: That is why! But there is more to the story. The old people say ... (*Looks about him as if he found somebody were listening*)

Peadar: Go on, Neelus. What do the old people say?

Neelus: The old people say that what you would think to be the wind crying is the sweet voice of lovely Sharon crying for her handsome young chieftain. They say that what you would think to be the wind blowing is the voice of Shíofra wailing and cursing in her misery.

Peadar: It is a sad story.

Neelus: (*Lonely*) It will be the same story always unless the bodies of two young men are cast into the hole. One will be small and ugly and wicked and the other will be tall and straight and pure like the noble chieftain.

Peadar: Is that part of the legend?

Neelus: 'Tis all in the story ... (*Turns to his father*) He's very bad ... my poor father, my poor father!

Peadar: With the fine days coming now, he'll improve. The fine weather is a great cure for all forms of sickness.

Neelus: (*Looks at Peadar vaguely*) The Banshee was crying last night over Baltavinn. I know the cry of the Banshee because it makes you shiver as if the cry was inside your ear. The last time the cry was heard, my mother died a few days after. God grant her a silver bed in heaven, my poor mother. (*Looks at his father*) He's that sick he doesn't know who are here and he doesn't know we are talking about him. That's very like death, that sickness.

Peadar: He's a long ways from being dead, Neelus.

Neelus: Did you ever hear the way Sharon cries in her grave in the quiet nights of summer?

Peadar: (*Doubtfully*) No!

Neelus: (*Cups his hands over his mouth and makes a whistling sound. Long drawn out and eerie. In the bed the old man stirs and moans faintly. In a panic, Neelus rushes to the left exit and calls loudly*) He cried out. Trassie! He stirred himself. He gave a moan out of him.

(*Peadar rises and stands anxiously. Enter Trassie. She hurries to the bed and bends over the old man. She takes his hand and feels his brow. Then she turns to Peadar*)

Trassie: It was nothing. The same as always. He is very weak in himself. He calls from time to time.

Peadar: Is he long ailing?

Trassie: This long time now. He got a fit a year ago. They said it was a stroke. He never rose from the bed since he took sick. This last week or so he is going from worse to worse. There isn't much a body can do.

Peadar: Is there no hope for him?

Trassie: He is too old to fight now!

Neelus: (*Draws near the bed, places his hand on his father's hand*) 'Tis when we'll all be asleep he'll go, the Lord save us! With no one to be near him. He'll be alone when he'll be called away into the caves (*Tone of awe*) and he'll be walking for ever and ever through the caves and he won't know where he's going and he'll be for ever and ever going deep down into the roundy caves and he'll never ...

Trassie: (*Gently*) Don't talk like that, Neelus. You know what will happen if you'll be talking like that. You'll be crying again and you won't be able to sleep. Stop it now, Neelus!

Neelus: (*Dejected tone*) 'Tis in the dark he'll come. Oh, he'll come like a fox and he'll sweep him away in a flash, my poor father.

Trassie: (*Firmly, gently*) Neelus, stop will you? You'll make trouble for all of us. (Puts her hand around his shoulders) Go down to the kitchen and wet the tea. The kettle is boiling. Go on now, Neelus a chroidhe. (*She gently manoeuvres him towards left exit*) You're a gift for making tea. (*She exits Neelus*)

Trassie: (*To Peadar*) What was he saying to you?

Peadar: Nothing you'd bother to carry with you.

Trassie: You needn't tell me. He talks of nothing else. He is a good-looking boy, a fine grádhbhar young fellow and the girls did take to him and they used to go with him, but somehow they run away from him now.

Peadar: I understand.

Trassie: I'm not denying he's a bit odd. But he was better than he is now.

Peadar: It's all right. I know what it is with him. No fault of his, the poor boy.

Trassie: Will you come to the kitchen and eat something now? You'll want something for the cold road.

Peadar: If you like me to, I'll sit a while and keep an eye on the old man. I don't mind. Many is the time I sat up with my own father when he was ailing ... I could stay. I wouldn't mind.

Trassie: (*Quickly, fearfully*) No! ... No! No need for you! Come to the kitchen. I'll stay here.

Peadar: Sorry if I am making too free. I meant well.

Trassie: And sorry myself to think I refused your kindness. But his people will be here shortly. (*Hesitantly*) They might take offence if they thought a stranger was attending him.

Peadar: You have somebody to relieve you, then?

Trassie: I have.

Peadar: Are they the one drop of blood?

Trassie: His brother's two sons, my first cousins. They come here every night, about this time, to see him.

Peadar: That's a pleasant thing to hear. That you have your own near you, when you want them.

(*Trassie frowns a little. Peadar, puzzled, looks at her*)

Peadar: When there is sickness in a house, your own will be the first to help you.

Trassie: You should be thinking of putting something in your stomach. Neelus forgets to keep the teapot warm.

Peadar: There was no need to go to so much trouble for me. (*Rises*) In pardon to you I'll go down, then.

(*Exit Peadar. Trassie seems to be about to call him back, but hesitates and folds her arms, worried. She tends to her father's comfort, leaves him and looks out the window, biting her lips, clutching her waist with her arms, pon-dering, turns, pats her father's forehead, waits a moment, and exits left, leaving the door but barely open. There is a sound of movement outside the front door. Very slowly the latch lifts and the door is pushed inward but nobody appears. After a few seconds what seems like a man with two heads appears in the doorway. They are two people, one carrying the other on his back. The man on the back moves and looks craftily over the other's shoulder, watching for movement in the room. The other looks stupidly about. The man on the back is Dinzie Conlee. The man carrying him is his brother Jack Conlee.*

Dinzie Conlee is of indeterminate age. His face is gruesome, twisted, as he looks about. He is slightly humped. A wizened small person, his legs paralysed.

The man Jack Conlee, on the other hand, is a large well-cut, well-proportioned man in his early twenties)

Dinzie: *(As he looks about)* Bring us in, Jack. Bring us in, boy! (Gives Jack a prod in the back)

Jack: *(Wincing)* Go aisy, Dinzie, can't you? ... Go aisy! You're always hurting me.

Dinzie: *(Ignoring Jack's feelings, goads him to the centre of the kitchen)* No one in, Jack! No one in! (He surveys the old man)

Jack: Trassie is out, Dinzie.

Dinzie: *(Always careful to ignore Jack's feelings)* Take us a-near the bed, Jack boy. Take us a-near the bed.

(Dutifully, Jack carries him to the bed. Dinzie leans over Jack's shoulder and surveys the old man)

Dinzie: Are you listening, Donal? ... Are you listening? ... (*Prods Jack*) Straighten, Jack! Straighten! You'll have me inside in the bed with him next. Are you paying heed, Donal? Wouldn't you die for yourself, wouldn't you? (*In anger*) Wouldn't you die, you old ropaire and not be keeping God waiting? (*To Jack, chuckling*) Maybe 'tis the Devil that's waiting for him.

Jack: (*Pleading*) Ah, don't, Dinzie, Don't! Leave him alone. He's our uncle!

Dinzie: (*Prods Jack on the back, and slaps the back of Jack's head so that Jack squirms*) On the table, Jack, boy. On the table. Or would you like to fly to the moon with me, and back? (*Chuckles*) On the table, Jack. Steady the blood! Woe, Pony!

(Jack backs Dinzie towards the table and puts him sitting on it, relieved of the weight, exercises his shoulder muscles, and approaches the bed to survey his uncle. Jack lies on floor and kicks his legs in the air like a horse. He snorts and whinnies before he rises)

Jack: Will he last long, Dinzie?

Dinzie: (*Shrewdly*) It can't be soon enough for me, Jack! Frightful blackguarding, keeping the whole country waiting. He's holding on for spite, Jack.

Jack: (*Pleads*) Ah, Dinzie, he's our uncle. 'Tisn't right to talk like that.

Dinzie: (*Shouts at the man in the bed*) Wouldn't you die for yourself and not be keeping us all dancing attendance on you?

(*Enter Trassie from left*)

Trassie: I heard the voices. I knew who it was. I was getting the tea.

Dinzie: Wouldn't you have a word of welcome for us, anyway? We aren't soupers!

Trassie: (*Pleasantly*) I'm sorry if I sounded the way you said, especially when ye come here every evening to see him.

Dinzie: (*Sanctimoniously*) There's no harm in us. We praises every-one as we go along. We keeps to ourselves. Don't we, Jack? ... I say, don't we Jack?

Jack: We do, Dinzie, we do.

Trassie: (*Indicating bed*) He's not good this evening.

Dinzie: We was praying all night for him. Jack said a pile of prayers, too. Didn't you, Jack? You should have heard Jack praying. His guts rumbles when he says his prayers. I say, didn't you, Jack?

Jack: Oh, I did! I did!

Trassie: Would you like a drop of tea?

Dinzie: You know it wasn't the tea that brought us, Trassie! I'm the kind of man that if I wanted tea, I'd ask up. We're not oul' women, Trassie. We never drink tea, except for our break-fast and supper.

Trassie: What brought you so?

Dinzie: Ah, now, Trassie, don't be trickin' with your own cousin. You know the thing we were talking about, don't you?

Trassie: (*Hotly*) I told you before, Dinzie Conlee, that I wouldn't even give ear to such a thing.

Dinzie: When the old man here die, Trassie ... when he die, I say, 'twould be the best thing if you moved yourself over into my father's house, where you'll be safe with your own people. (*Quickly*) The country is crawling with villains and lads that do be watching lone women with a thought for catching them. They'd put you down on a floor in a minute and go across you.

Trassie: (*Indignantly*) With Neelus in the house, who would bother me? Neelus will stay as long as I'm here.

Dinzie: (*Mock sadness*) But, sure, you won't be here, Trassie, my little jewel. Won't you be over sitting down by my father's hearth and the whole house-full of them bringing you tea and leaving you in bed in the cold mornings.

Trassie: You'd better be going home now, Dinzie. This is my house and Neelus' house, and here we'll stay, and we want no one here but ourselves.

Dinzie: (*As if he had not heard*) You'll be like a queen there with my father telling you stories and my mother tending to your every want and Jack here breaking the hasp of his behind to give you comfort. Tell her, Jack!

Jack: Yerra, Dinzie, I'm no good for explaining.

Dinzie: You don't know the life you'd have. Jack will be up early ... (*Shouts at Jack*) Jack!

Jack: That's right.

Dinzie: (*Soft voice*) Jack will be out of his bed with the first light of day to bring in musharoons for your breakfast and when the water be low in the warm weather he'll be capturing white trout for you. We kills four pigs in the one year and think of the puddings and pork steak frying for you and your own cut off every flitch that hangs from the ceiling.

Trassie: If you don't go home and stop your cross talk, I'll call in the dogs out of the yard to scold you.

Dinzie: (*Unperturbed*) I wouldn't like to be you, Trassie, when the old man dies, with no one ...

Trassie: (*Resolute*) I'll have Neelus here with me and I want to hear no more about your house or about your father and mother or about Jack .... (*Jack squirms*) Oh, Jack, you're a man without a mind to let that devil control you. Wouldn't you give a buck jump some day below near Carraig Head and fire him away out into the sea, or wouldn't you find a nice girl and make a marriage bed for yourself?

Jack: The weather'll be getting too warm soon for marriage, Trassie.

Dinzie: (*Calmly*) Don't mind her, Jack! She's only trying to come between us, between two brothers .... two out of the one litter.

Trassie: Wouldn't you go home, Dinzie? Jack, wouldn't you take him up on your back and let my father die in peace. Carry him with you, Jack, out of here!

Dinzie: (*In a rage, strikes the table with his fists*) I won't go out of here! ... I won't go out of here! I have no legs to be travel-ling the country with. I must have my own place. (*Violent rage*) I do be crying and cursing myself at night in bed because no woman will talk to me. I puts my nails to my flesh (*Grits teeth with temper*) because no girl will ever look at me on account of my dead legs. (*Then indicates his back*) And this impostor here, (*Wrathfully tries to claw the hump on his back*) this hound of the devil, this curse o' God on my back.

Jack: You'll give yourself a fit, Dinzie. We'll go now.

Dinzie: (*Fiercely*) We won't go. My father promised me this place would be mine, and it will be mine. She'll go home to our house. What do she want with a house of her own and land and cattle besides? What do she want with it, when she has no notion of marrying, herself?

Trassie: Close your mouth!

Dinzie: (*Beats upon the table*) I will not close my mouth! (*Opens his mouth pitifully, says sadly*) When I was fourteen years of age I used to be thinking of girls ... thinking I was then and thinking I am now ... and thinking I'll be for the rest of my living days unless I have a house and land to draw women to me.

Trassie: Close up and go! Go now, Dinzie Conlee and leave us alone!

Dinzie: (*Absently*) Will I sing, Jack? I say, Jack, will I sing? (*To Trassie*) I have black teeth, but I have beautiful gums. I can't sing? But I can hum like a honey bee.

Trassie: Are you going to take him, Jack, or will I call in the dogs?

Jack: (*Defensively, weakly*) Sure, if I put him up on my back now he'll kill me with the pucking he'll give me. Wouldn't you be said by him, Trassie, and stay over with us. L'ave him here an' he'll get some oul' woman. 'Twill satisfy him.

Dinzie: Be said by Jack, Trass! Be said by him! Jack is as sound as the tar road you'd be walking on, Jack looks like an ass, Trassie, but he's a pony in his heart. Aren't you, Jack?

Jack: (*Modestly*) Ah, Dinzie!

(Enter Peadar Minogue, from the left)

Peadar: (*Politely salutes the newcomers and addresses Trassie*) How is he now?

Trassie: No sign of a change in him. He's still the way he was.

Dinzie: (*Accusing*) Who's he? Who's he, I say? Who's he, Jack?

Threaten him, Jack! Ask him who he is, with his head bare in a strange house. Go on, Jack!

Jack: (*Draws himself up to his full dimensions*) What's your name?

Peadar: My name is Peadar Minogue.

Jack: (*Reflects stupidly for a second*) Why so are you here?

Peadar: I'm a journeyman thatcher.

Dinzie: (*Chuckles*) Could you put a thatch on a baldy head? What call have you to be here? Ask him what call he has to be here, Jack. Go on, Jack.

Jack: What call have you to be here?

Peadar: Searching for work only. I was passing the road by and saw the thatch rotten on this house and I said to myself 'twould be as gay for me to call.

Dinzie: I never heard of the name Minogue in these parts!

Peadar: I'm only going the road looking for work.

Dinzie: The best thing you could do would be to keep on going the road.

Peadar: That's my intention.

Dinzie: Fellows like you upset me, leaving the road, going into houses, looking for bread and meat.

Peadar: I work for what I eat and I always did that same.

Dinzie: You have the look of a man who never had the full of his belly!

Peadar: If 'tis insults you want to cast, cast them! I'm a black stranger here. I mean no harm.

Dinzie: (*Anger*) There was more thrown to dogs in our house than was eat in yours in the round of a year!

Peadar: We were never hungry, and any man that struck the dinner in our house was never hungry.

Dinzie: Who's to say? Every fool will boast about his table. In my house when myself and Jack sit down facing each other there is that mound o' meat and spuds between us that we can't see each other 'atin!

Trassie: (*To Peadar*) Maybe you'd be wanting to wash yourself before you go. You'll find a bucket of water on the small table near the dresser. There's a towel hanging about it.

Peadar: A wash would do no harm.

(*Peadar exits left, looking curiously at the company in the room*)

Dinzie: The house will be alive with fleas after him!

Trassie: He doesn't look that way. He's as clean as you.

Dinzie: D'you hear that, Jack. D'you hear the way she's black-guarding your brother?

Jack: (*Half-hearted*) Ah, leave her alone, can't ye.

Dinzie: (*Points finger at sick man in bed*) He won't be long more in the world, Trassie. They're calling him now and he won't go. When he goes you'll be coming over to our house and we'll send Neelus off to the home. (*Trassie makes to protest*) Will you let me talk, Trassie; will you let a poor oul' cripple talk; will you let your own cousin talk? Why do they be all plaguing me, Jack? Trassie, this is the way of it. When your father die, my father will give him a good wake and funeral – won't he, Jack?

Jack: My father said it all right, Trass! He said he'd buy four firkins of porter and a dozen of wine and whiskey and the dearest coffin in the town of Lenamore.

Dinzie: (*Quickly, as Trassie is about to interrupt*) I will come here then to this place, and I'll find some oul' woman to marry me. (*Pitifully*) Sure, I sees the girls going to chapel every Sunday. They do be lovely with their long hair jumping up and down on their shoulders and their fleshy collops so daintily walking the road. (*Hits the table again*) I must have a girl to marry me.

Jack: Go aisy, Dinzie, or you'll upset yourself.

Dinzie: (*Shrieks loudly*) Stop telling me to go aisy! Stop will you, or I'll stick you! 'Tis fine for you that can walk into a dance-hall and catch hold of a woman and dance with her. (*Challenge*) Will you swap backs with me? Will you knock this villain of the Devil's breed from between my shoulders.

Jack: Your turn will come, Dinzie. 'Twill come in time.

Dinzie: Don't be teasing. Jack, don't be teasing.

(*The old man stirs in the bed*)

Trassie: Wouldn't the two of ye go away home or ye'll wake up my father.

Dinzie: What does he want waking up for, wouldn't he stay the way he is?

Trassie: Take Dinzie home, Jack, or your uncle will wake.

Jack: Come on away, Dinzie. We'll come back again.

Dinzie: 'Come on away, Dinzie'; 'Come home, Dinzie!' Ye're all ag'in me. Have I no feelings at all? Do I see or feel nothing? Which of ye know what I feel ... I watches the lads with their girls over on the strand near Carraig Head in the height of summer. I sees the big mountainy farmers galloping like stud horses through the shallow water and they dragging their girls after them through the spray. Is it how you think I don't notice the way a drop o' water do be shining on the white milky flesh of a young woman?

Jack: Ah, Dinzie, 'tis only bringing tortures on yourself you are.

Dinzie: I see the handsome young girls and they casting warm looks of longing over the young men and I know what they do be thinking, but none of them cares about giving an eye to Dinzie Conlee. (Sincerely) What harm but I would be fonder of a girl than any one of 'em. I would mind her the same as a child and give over to every wish she'd put to me.

Jack: Ah, Dinzie, 'tis only yourself you're hurtin'!

Dinzie: (*Unaware*) I would leave no one say a single word to her in crossness. I would polish and shine her shoes for her like the black of a crow's wing. I would cut her toenails and wash her feet for her in the evening. Oh, I would give in to her no matter what she would say, so long as she would come into my bed at night and hear out the end of my troubles and we could be whispering to each other the small things of the day. (*Shakes fist at the old man in the bed*) Wouldn't you give over, you oul' pizawn, wouldn't you die and have done with it?

(*The old man stirs in the bed, rises on an elbow and opens his eyes. Trassie rushes to assist him. The old man, helped by Trassie, sits up in the bed, looks at Dinzie and tries to speak. He stammers at Dinzie who recoils a little. He raises his right hand in threatening attitude towards Dinzie who recoils further. The old man then falls back against Trassie's hands. She lays him on the bed*)

Trassie: Will you have no pity for a sick old man? Will you see my father dying and have no consideration for him?

(*She lays him gently again on the pillows*)

Dinzie: (*Assured that the old man is helpless, lifts his fists towards the bed in fighting attitude and shouts*) Come on! ... Come on, I say! ... Come on, let you! I'm not afraid of you. (*Viciously points his finger at the old man*) We'll beat him, Jack. Did you see him pointing at me, Jack?

Trassie: (*Tearfully*) 'Tis you that should be in the home, not Neelus. Are you taking leave of your senses altogether? My father is dying! Jack, take that brother you have and carry him home to his room and shut him in from all of us.

Dinzie: (*Indignantly*) D'you hear her, Jack? D'you hear what she's saying about your own brother?(*Gently*) Put me up on your back, Jack. Put me up on your back, my own brother.

Jack: (*Hopefully*) Are we going home, Dinzie?

Dinzie: (*Shrieks*) We won't go home! We won't go home! Put me up on your back, Jack. Put me up on your back 'till I attack her.

Jack: The last time you struck a body was at Lenamore Fair and I gave twenty-eight days in jail for you. If you strike Trassie, Dinzie, it might be worse .... (*Menace*) ... If you strike the old man they'll have it that you killed him and 'tis me they'll hang, Dinzie. I'll take no more blame for you. I'd hate to hang from a rope for any man. I won't dangle for you Dinzie. I won't dangle.

(*Dinzie thumps the table viciously and scowls*)

I didn't mean that, Dinzie, 'pon my soul and conscience, but come on away home. Can't you come on. They'll be won-dering what's holding us here all night.

Dinzie: All right, Jack, we'll go! (*Warningly to Trassie*) No more of your nonsense now. I won't have it from you. The minute he's put into his trench I'll be making my way over here. Have your clothes bundled and ready. Put me up, Jack. Put me up and carry me home. (*Jack hoists him on to his back*)

Jack: Have you a grip? Get a good grip.

Dinzie: (*Putting his arms around Jack's neck*) Right, Jack! Right, Jack! Steady, boy! (*To Trassie*) Send word over by Neelus if he takes a turn for the worse.

Trassie: Ye'll have word.

Dinzie: Go on, pony! Go on! (*Clicks his tongue*)

Jack: I told you not to be calling me pony.

Dinzie: Right, Jack! Right, Jack! Right, Boy! (*As if he were addressing a pony, clicks his tongue*) Go on! Go on!

(*Jack opens the door and exits with Dinzie. Trassie stands perplexed after their departure. As she does so, Peadar enters from the left*)

Trassie: Did you eat enough?

Peadar: I had plenty, thanks.

Trassie: Where will you go now?

Peadar: To the west. The men will be busy now with the fishing and there's sure to be work.

Trassie: Have you people of your own anywhere?

Peadar: I have a brother, married, with a small farm in the moun-tains. I spend the winters there. If I had my bag now, I'd be going.

(*Trassie exits and returns with the bag. She places it on the floor*)

Trassie: Where will you sleep the night?

Peadar: I'll find a place – maybe a hay shed or an old stable.

Trassie: But how will you sleep without clothes over you? There is cold in the wind, and wet, too, in it from the sea. You would be frozen.

Peadar: I'm well used to it. (*Sincerely*) I was often frozen to the heart, sleeping without shelter.

Trassie: Have you been to the west before?

Peadar: Not as far as this.

Trassie: It is far different from the mountains where you will find shelter. There is no shade here, only the hard wind blowing in to you. It would go through your clothes and sting you.

Peadar: (*Stooping to pick up his bag*) I'll find some place.

Trassie: Wait ... maybe ... maybe you could sleep here if you weren't afraid to sleep with Neelus.

Peadar: Why should I be afraid?

Trassie: Sometimes he goes out and might not come back 'till morning.

Peadar: Where does he go?

Trassie: Down to Carraig Head to have a look at the sea. The full moon and the high tide is the worst time for him or when the peal salmon run in the first days of summer. He acts queerly then.

Peadar: What harm is that?

Trassie: It is not right to be wandering around in the night. (*Then in a tone which has some appeal*) Would you sleep with him and not notice him?

Peadar: I wouldn't notice him. I sleep sound. I would be very thankful for the chance of a bed.

Trassie: You could start away with the first light tomorrow. We rise early here.

Peadar: Do you keep milch cows?

Trassie: We have seven, three calving. We have a few head of sheep. They graze the open mountain that falls into the sea.

(*Enter Neelus from the left. He surveys his father*)

Neelus: Did they go – Dinzie and Jack?

Trassie: They've gone.

Neelus: Why don't you lock the door on them, Trassie. Lock the door and they can't come in.

Trassie: They're your cousins, Neelus. I couldn't do that.

Neelus: (*Fearfully*) I know what they want to do with me. I hear them talking. They want to drive me away from here – away from Carraig Head and the salt water. Where you would see no seagull against the black of the cliffs. Where you would never hear the cannon guns in the caves.

Trassie: No! No! No! Neelus ... I won't let them do that! I would never see you sent away like that. I would never let them touch my boy – my own dear boy.

Neelus: (*Looking around him fearfully, hands to sides*) I know Dinzie Conlee. He hates me. He hates you, Trassie. He'll hunt me away from Carraig Head and the tides. (*Fearfully*) I won't see the fingers of the silvery tide feeling the goldy sands before she throws her body down on it. I'll choke and smother in the black room. They'll hunt you, too, Trassie. Dinzie Conlee is the Devil!

Trassie: (*Touches his hand consolingly*) We will always stay here, Neelus ... the two of us.

Neelus: (*Faraway look*) Dinzie and Jack will hunt you, too, Trassie. (*He looks helplessly at Trassie*) What will I do, Trassie?

Trassie: (*Looks at Peadar*) He's trying to help me, but his mind is bothered. (*Neelus nods helplessly*)

Peadar: Why should you want help? Is there something wrong? Can I do anything to help?

Trassie: No! ... Nothing! (*Hastily*) You mustn't take notice of what he says. Talk to him for a while. I'll go to fix your bed.

(*Trassie looks at her father and exits*)

Peadar: What did you mean when you said Dinzie and Jack would hunt your sister? (*Waits for reply. Receives none*) What did you mean when you said it? There must be something bad in store for the two of you. You wouldn't want to see Trassie hurted, would you? Think, Neelus, of what you were saying a while back. Think of Trassie.

Neelus: Trassie ... (*Vaguely*) ... Trassie ... (Gently) ... Trassie.

Peadar: Yes, Trassie! You wouldn't like if she were hurted, Neelus.

Neelus: (*Awesome*) Below in Sharon's grave where they do be crying ... below in the deep wet black of the cold rocks ...

Peadar: (*Touching Neelus' arm with his hand, says considerately*) No, Neelus! Think! (*Pauses, reflects*) We will follow each other with talk out into the night. I will tell you about the singing finches in Glashnanaon, my country and then, maybe, you'll tell me about yourself and Trassie in your own childish time.

(*Curtain*)

ACT ONE
SCENE II

The action takes place in the same room as before. The time is the late evening of two days later.

The room is changed – in as much as there are now several chairs in it.

On the bed the old man lies dead. He is facing the audience slightly propped up. He is dressed in a brown habit. The bed is made neatly underneath him. The uppermost clothes are white.

Brass candlesticks, holding lighted candles, stand on a table. There is also a saucer filled with snuff, on the table.

A prayer-book props the old man's head up. A rosary beads is entwined in his hands.

Neelus – dressed in a new suit of coarse quality, stiff collar and new brown boots – stands near the closed door, hands behind his back. He walks towards the bed, looks at the old man, and turns again to the door, standing impatiently, hands behind his back. He continually screws up his face and admires his new clothes with his hands.

There is a subdued knock at the door. Neelus is alert immediately. He lifts the latch and stands aside.

Enter two women, one tall and one small. The tall one is a cadaverous, sad-looking person; the other short and stout and of a nosy disposition – both in their middle fifties. They are followed by an old man, Tom Shaun.

The tall woman is Moll, the small woman Mague. Both shake hands with Neelus sympathetically. Tom Shaun shakes the

*hand of Neelus and lays another on his shoulder. Tom Shaun is
aided by a walking stick.*

Mague: What time did he die, the poor man?

Neelus: Last night late.

Mague: Had he a lot of pain?

Neelus: No! No pain! He only left a little gasp out of him.

Mague: (*To Moll*) Wasn't he lucky to have no pain?

Moll: He was blessed.

Mague: (*To Neelus*) Did he say anything an' he dyin'?

Neelus: He did! He said, 'God take me out of my misery!'

(Both women sigh sympathetically)

Mague: Any more?

Neelus: He said we'd get rain in the course of a few days ...
I have his watch. (*Takes silver watch from his pocket
and fondles it*) Trassie gave it to me. It loses three
minutes in the day.

(The women shake their heads sorrowfully and advance to the bed)

Moll: Ah! God bless him, isn't he a handsome corpse!

Mague: He's lovely, the fine decent man.

Moll: That had a hard word for no one.

Mague: That would give you the bite he'd be eatin'.

(Moll feels the quality of the cloth of the habit and says to Mague)

Moll: The best of material.

(Both take pinches of snuff, apply it to their noses, and survey the room)

Moll: *(To Neelus)* Where's Trassie?

Neelus: She's feeding the men in the kitchen.

Moll: Is there many of them there?

Mague: Did your cousins from Luascawn come?

Moll: What about your mother's people from Lenamore?

(Neelus does not reply but goes forward and holds the watch to the ears of the women, and Tom Shaun)

Neelus: D'you hear the little heart thumping inside?

(Neelus returns to the door. The two women exchange meaningful glances. Both kneel, bless themselves and commence to pray. They then take their places alongside two other women already seated from the beginning of the scene. All four women pay out their beads through their fingers and whisper decades of the rosary to themselves. Neelus holds the watch to his ear, smiling. A knock at the door, Neelus lifts the latch and stands aside. Two more old women enter and follow the procedure of Moll and Mague. When all six women are seated they take up a low and mournful keening which Neelus is fascinated with. Enter Trassie with Peadar, the

43

latter bearing a tray of filled tea cups which Trassie distributes to the old women. Peadar remains at a distance and is joined by Neelus. When the opportunity presents itself the women keen and lament)

Neelus: They're all looking at you, Peadar, wondering who you are and where you came from.

(Tom Shaun lights his pipe)

(Peadar turns and looks calmly at the women)

That's Peadar Minogue, the thatcher. He sleeps in the one bed with me. (*Proudly*) He hails from Glashnanaon where the singing birds do be. He tells me all about the singing birds before we go to sleep.

Woman 1: You're welcome to these parts, Sir.

Peadar: Thank you kindly.

Tom Shaun: Would you, by any chance, be anything to the Minogues of Tooreentubber that used to keep the boar?

Peadar: I have heard tell of them but there's no relationship between us.

Tom Shaun: The Minogue bonhams were as hardy as terriers. There was a piebald in every litter.

Peadar: No, there's no relation.

Tom Shaun: There was a Minogue, now, a small block of a man, a thatcher, too, by the same token – Thomas

Timmy Minogue they used to call him. He married into six cows in Glounsharoon. He used travel to Aonachmore pattern in a common car. A jinnet he had and the white knight we used to call him. That same jinnet was a born gentleman. (*Having divested herself of this, Woman 2 lights a pipe. The formal atmosphere relaxes as the women quiz Peadar*)

Peadar: I heard tell of him, too, but we're not connected.

Woman 1: (*Brightly*) What would your mother's name be now? Is she alive or dead?

Peadar: She's dead this long time, the Lord ha' mercy on her. From Errimore, a Hennessy.

Tom Shaun: (*Reflectively*) Hennessys from Errimore, Hennessys from Errimore. Hennessys. There was a Timmineen Hennessy, a flamin' stepdancer, from the Errimore side. Would they be the one Hennessys?

Peadar: Timmineen Hennessy was my grand-uncle.

Tom Shaun: Glory be to us all, but isn't it a small world. (*Looks around for proof*) and you tell me Timmineen Hennessy was your grand-uncle? Sure, his feet were like forks of lightning. He would dance on a three-penny bit for you. Have you any step yourself?

Peadar: I can dance a hornpipe.

Tom Shaun: Kind for you to be able! Kind for you !
(*Reflectively in wonder*) And Timmineen Hennessy
to be your grand-uncle. Was there ever better than
that?

(*Trassie takes tray and goes towards the exit. She turns*)

Trassie: (*To Neelus*) Will you come to the kitchen and have
something to eat?

Neelus: I want to stay here at the door.

Trassie: You can eat later on. (*To Peadar*) Will I bring you
something to drink?

Peadar: Thank you ... but I have no mind for it.

Trassie: You must be tired – up all night, with no sleep.

Peadar: Glad to give a hand only.

Trassie: Maybe you would like to go out in the air. It would
put new life into you.

Peadar: I'll walk a little ways, so.

(*Peadar goes towards the door where Neelus is, watched closely by
the seated women. Neelus opens the door for him. Exit Peadar.
Trassie exits left*)

Moll: (*To Mague*) There was a Banshee heard calling over
the inches last night.

Mague: Notice in plenty.

Tom Shaun: (*Who up to this has not spoken*) There was an ould bard of a tomcat with whiskers like needles by him, crying over the inches last night.

Moll: (*To Mague*): The Banshee gave three long cries of torment every while.

Tom Shaun: (*To no one in particular*) This ould whiskery tomcat used to leave three lonesome cries out of him every while.

Moll: (*Angrily*) For a finish there was one long terrible cry and then no more.

Tom Shaun: For a wind up didn't this ould cat leave one long terrible cry out of him, that you would hear in the other world. Calling, he was, for his little pussy and she never came to him. You'd swear it was the Banshee that was crying but it was only an oul' whiskery tomcat.

(*Moll gives the woman a withering look*)

People do be easily fooled. I'm goin' to the kitchen for a drop of the hot stuff. (*He exits. Tom Shaun returns at once with whiskey*)

(*The women now keen unrestrainedly, tear their hair and comfort themselves*)

(*There is a knock at the door. Neelus lifts the latch and stands aside. Enter a well-dressed woman in her forties. She walks as if she owned the world. Her accent is precise. She shakes hands with*

Neelus and kneels by the bed in prayer. She is the local schoolmistress, Miss Dee. There is respect-ful silence while she prays, broken only by Neelus who takes a pinch of snuff. Miss Dee rises and sits on a chair near the main door and alongside Woman 1)

Miss Dee: Good evening, everybody!

Moll & Mague: (*Ingratiatingly*) Good evening, Miss Dee.

Miss Dee: (*To Tom Shaun*) Must you smoke when a man is dead?

(Tom Shaun quickly puts the pipe away. Neelus comes forward and holds the watch to Miss Dee's ear. She strikes his hand violently. Frightened, Neelus returns to the door)

Miss Dee: (*To Neelus*) Where is Trassie?

> (*Neelus hangs his head*)

> (*Firmly*) Don't try to fool me, boy. I know what goes on in your head. You're not half as simple as people think. Where is your sister? (*Neelus points a finger towards the kitchen*) Do you mean she's in the kitchen? (*Neelus nods*) And why don't you say so? Making signs as if you were dumb.

Woman 1: (*Meekly*) And how are all your scholars, Miss Dee?

Miss Dee: They are not my scholars, my good woman. I merely teach them.

(The women nod in agreement)

Miss Dee: (*Turns to Moll and Mague*) What in heaven's name are you nodding at? If you have something to say, say it. I fancy if that poor man on his death-bed could say something, he would, and be very glad if he could.

Neelus: I know who's coming now! (*Puts his ear to the door*) I know who's coming now!

Miss Dee: Whatever are you talking about?

Neelus: My cousins, Jack and Dinzie.

Miss Dee: (*A little anxiously*) How do you know?

Neelus: Because I know the heavy fall of Jack's feet from carrying Dinzie.

(*Suddenly there is a loud knocking at the door. Neelus stands well back. The latch lifts and the door opens*)

Dinzie: (*From without*) Go on, Jack, boy! Go on, pony!

(*Enter Jack, carrying Dinzie on his back. Jack shakes hands with Neelus. Neelus puts the watch to Jack's ear, then to Dinzie's. Dinzie snatches the watch and puts it into his own pocket. Neelus stands cowed, hands covering his head*)

Go on over to the bed Jack. Go on.

(*Jack carries Dinzie to the bed*)

Bend over him 'till we see is he dead.

(*Jack leans forward. Dinzie touches the corpse lightly*)

(*To corpse*) Are you dead, Donal? Are you dead, I say? Look at the face of him, Jack. Are you dead, Donal, I say? Will you have me talking to myself? Is he dead, Jack?

Jack: (*Placatingly*) Oh, wisha, Dinzie, he's dead all right. Leave him alone and don't be tormenting him.

Dinzie: Go on Jack. Go around 'till we see who's here.

(Jack takes Dinzie around)

Dinzie: (*To Moll and Mague*) What business have ye here? A nice pair of old hags, snuffin' an' gossipin' an' drinkin' yeer little sups of tay an' cuttin' an' backbitin' everybody.

(Jack carries him to where Miss Dee sits)

Dinzie: Who left you in?

Miss Dee: I came to pay my respects to the dead.

Dinzie: You came spyin' to see who was here. Why don't you get an oul' man for yourself an' get married?

Miss Dee: How dare you!

Dinzie: (*Mimicking her voice*) How dare you! How dare you!

Miss Dee: You should be on your knees, praying for your dead uncle.

Dinzie: Should I, now?

Miss Dee: Yes, you should, and show a little respect for the
dead.

Dinzie: (*In a rage*) Give her a lick of a fist, Jack.

Jack: Ah, can't you go aisy, Dinzie! Isn't it a wake-room
we're in!

Dinzie: Go on, give her a lick! She used to give me slaps at
school long ago when I usen't know my tables. She
used to give a poor oul' cripple slaps. (*Pretends to cry
most unholy, lunatic wailing and weeping*)

Miss Dee: (*Viciously*) You richly deserved every slap you got.
You were the wickedest boy in the school. I didn't
slap you half enough.

Dinzie: Oh, good God, Jack, are you going to let her talk to
a poor defenceless cripple like that? Ketch her by
the throat, Jack, and give her a squeeze.

Jack: But sure you well know I can't, Dinzie. We'd have
the law on top of us. I went to jail before for you,
Dinzie. I know what 'tis like.

Dinzie: Only for a month! Only for a month, Jack. And
wasn't it worth it?

Jack: Are you going to sit down at all?

Dinzie: You're mad to be rid of me. (*Shouts at Neelus*)
Who's below in the kitchen?

Neelus: (*Fearfully*) A crowd of men drinkin' and 'ating.

Dinzie: (*To Jack*) Come on down and we'll rise a row with some-one.

Jack: (*Pleads*) Ah, can't you stop. Isn't it a wake-night? Wait until we're going home.

Dinzie: Frightful scampin' coming to examine a dead man and spillin' porter all over the house. A wake house is worse than a public house. We'll ketch some fellow half drunk and we'll give him a most unmerciful pucking goin' home.

Jack: Will you sit down now for a while? My back is achin' with the pain.

Dinzie: Put me down, Jack boy. Put me down, let you.

Jack: Where will you sit, Dinzie?

Dinzie: Put me down there Jack, where I can keep an eye on all of 'em.

(Jack places Dinzie on a chair where he commands a view of all. Jack goes through the motions of exercising his cramped muscles. Dinzie pulls his legs up under him in the chair. Jack goes through his exercises on the floor. The keening begins anew, more restrained. Dinzie listens piously for awhile and raises a hand)

Dinzie: (*Surveying crowd*) The quarest lookin' bart of weeds I ever witnessed. Wouldn't ye go away for yeerselves and not be annoying the poor man in the bed.

Miss Dee: You'll answer for your sins yet.

Dinzie: What do you want me to do? Start screeching and roaring with sorrow an' pull the hair out of my head in lumps.

Miss Dee: You are to be pitied! Can't you at least keep silent in the presence of death?

(This only serves to goad Dinzie on)

Dinzie: Jack, are you listening? I say, are you listening, Jack?

Jack: I am, Dinzie.

Dinzie: Do you know what I'm going to do when I die, Jack? Will I tell you?

Jack: (*Resignedly*) Go on, Dinzie! Tell me!

Dinzie: Well, Jack, when I be stretched out dead in my bed with a brown shirt on me like the lad here and my face the colour of limestone, I'll send the orders beforehand to Coolnaleen townland for Nell Keown, the concertina player, and I'll get about fourteen fiddlers from all over the parish and I'll have all of 'em playin' at my wake. I'll have porter to swim in and whiskey in tanks and I'll poison half the parish with drink. (*Laughs*) That'll be the sport, Jack, I'll have geese, Jack – roast geese, and male and rolled oats for this gang here. (*Points to Miss Dee*) We'll get a ladder for her and put her sittin' on top of it where she can see all. (*To Miss Dee*) Will you come? Ah, you will! Ah, you will! You'll come all right. Sure, there'd be no sport at all without you. (*Plucky, violently mischievous*) Ah, do, say you'll come. Say you'll come. 'Twould be no good being dead if your puss wasn't facing me. (*Changed tone*) I swear I'd wake up and give a roar at you and carry you screechin' to the coffin with me.

Miss Dee: If it wasn't for the respect I have for the dead, I'd leave here this instant minute.

Dinzie: Do you know what you must do, Jack, when I'm dead? You must pull a thick ashplant and put it beside me in the coffin and when they're shoulderin' me to the church yard, Jack, I'll hit the cover of the coffin a kick and knock it off ...

Jack: Ah, stop, Dinzie!

Dinzie: And sit up inside o' my coffin and flake the four polls of the livin' bastards that's carrying me to my grave.

Miss Dee: The curse of God attend you!

Dinzie: I told you, Jack, you should have given her a kick. (*Threat to Miss Dee*) Would you give me a slap now for not knowing my tables? One and one is two. Two and two is two. Three and two is two. Two and one is nine. Come on, give me a slap! (*Slowly*) If you give me a slap now, I'd hang for you, woman!

(*Enter Trassie*)

Dinzie: Will you be ready to go after the funeral tomorrow?

Trassie: Will you take something, Jack ... a drop o' whiskey?

Jack: I'll chance it.

Dinzie: Don't give me the deaf ear, Trassie, I won't take it from you. By God! I won't. You can be ready to go tomorrow evening.

Trassie: (*Notices Miss Dee*) Oh, Miss Dee! I didn't see you. Will I bring you something?

Dinzie: Bring her a fist of oats and a gábhail of hay. She's braying there with hunger since she landed.

Trassie: A drop o' wine?

Miss Dee: Just a little drop, if you please. (*Trassie exits*)

Dinzie: (*Loudly, boastfully*) I'll have my heels up on the hob of this hearth tomorrow night and maybe a woman of my own after a while. Jack, you'll be the best man at my wedding. I'll be well catered for. I'll have good times presently. I say, Jack, I'll have good times.

Jack: You're fond of yourself, Dinzie.

Dinzie: (*Wonder*) Fond of myself! I like myself Jack – every man likes himself, Jack, hump or no hump. I knew a fellow once going with a girl and he was fond of himself. (*Pauses reflectively*) He was so fond of himself that every time he'd give her a rub, usen't he to give himself a rub too.

Miss Dee: (*To Moll*) How's your husband keeping, these times?

Moll: (*Delighted to be asked*) Oh, he's fine, thank you.

Miss Dee: (*To Mague*) And you, Mrs Hallissey! How's your son in America?

Mague: Oh, he's going great entirely. He sends home ten dollars every week.

Miss Dee: Isn't he a good boy to do that?

Mague: (*Proudly*) Every week of his life he sends it. I get my envelope every single Monday morning from Jotty King, the postboy, with the ten dollars pasted inside and he sends a great bundle of money at Christmas, too.

Dinzie: (*Triumphantly, to nobody in particular*) Isn't that more of it an' they'd be bla-guardin' me for wanting a wife. Sure, isn't it well known that the postboy wasn't near her door in the space of five years since the shop-keepers got tired of sending her bills for the meal and flour she owes. (*Smiling to the ceiling*) God help us! They do be boasting about their sons and about the money they get. (*Tone of impeachment – to Mague*) Wouldn't you tell the truth. 'He sends you home ten dollars every week!'

He sends you home nothing! Ye spend yeer days
slaving for yeer sons and go into debt to send them
to America. And what do they do when they land
in America? Forget about ye. And aren't they right,
too? Isn't it a blessing in itself to get away from ye.

Miss Dee: Have you no consideration for the feelings of
other people?

Dinzie: Give us a song, Jack! Go on, Jack, give us a song – a
lonesome one.

*(Enter Trassie with drinks on a tray. She hands same to Jack and
Miss Dee. Jack swallows his in one gulp. Miss Dee sips genteely)*

Trassie: A biscuit, Miss Dee?

Miss Dee: No, thank you, Trassie. I don't care for sweet
things.

Dinzie: Are you going to ask me to have anything? Is it
how you think I have no mouth. Firing drink into
black strangers and leaving your own flesh and
blood go dry!

Trassie: You know what happens to you when you take
drink?

Dinzie: Nothing happens to me ... nothing ... nothing. Ye're
all down on me.

Trassie: You're welcome to what we have in the house, but
drink only sets you stone mad altogether.

(Exit Trassie)

Dinzie: *(To Neelus)* Come over here!

(Neelus advances timidly)

> *(Taking watch from pocket)* Do you want your watch back?

Neelus: *(Nods fervently)* I do! ... I do! ...

Dinzie: Right you are, so! ... down with you to the kitchen and the first bottle of whiskey you clap your eyes on, put it under your coat and bring it up to me. Mind you let no one catch you, or I'll dance on top of your watch.

(Neelus hurries to the kitchen)

Moll: *(Rises)* 'Tis time we were going home, Mague, girl.

Dinzie: What's your hurry? Yerra, sit down a while and rest your-self. Sure, aren't you going all day. Go on, sit down a while.

(Doubtfully Moll sits, Neelus hurries in and produces a partly-filled bottle of whiskey, triumphantly, from under his coat. He hands it to Dinzie and extends his hand for his watch. Dinzie shakes hands with him and drinks with relish from the bottle)

> Cock-a-doodle-doo!

(He swallows lengthily again, puts the bottle on the ground and rubs his hands together with delight. He motions to Neelus as if

he would whisper with him. He whispers something into his ear. Neelus nods understanding and hurries out by the front door)

Jack: What did you put him up to now, Dinzie?

Dinzie: (*Drinking from bottle*) Cock-a-doodle-doo! ... Cock-a-doodle-doo! ...

Jack: Ah, what did you tell him to do, Dinzie?

Dinzie: Soon enough we'll know, Jack.

Jack: Ah, can't you tell us, Dinzie?

Dinzie: 'Twill make a good year for hay ... I say, 'twill make a good year for hay, Jack.

Miss Dee: I hope you haven't put that poor boy up to any mischief.

Dinzie: Out for a gallop I sent him, to loosen him out.

Jack: Ah, Dinzie, you're a fright, you are!

Miss Dee: If you put that poor simple boy up to anything bad, God will visit you for it.

Dinzie: We'll have the kettle on for him when he comes!

(All the women assume shocked expressions, sighs of hor-ror, etc.)

Dinzie: (*Drinks from the bottle again*) Cock-a-doodle-doo! ... Cock-a-doodle-doo ... doo ... dooo ... (*Shrieks of laughter*)

(Enter Neelus by the front door. He goes immediately to Dinzie.

He has something under his coat. First he extends his hand to Dinzie for the watch. Dinzie hands him the watch and Neelus takes a leather whip from under his coat and hands it to Dinzie. Dinzie accepts it and puts the bottle aside)

Jack: What's that for, Dinzie?

Dinzie: Not for you, Jack! Did I ever use a whip on you, Jack?

Jack: No, but you often threatened me!

Dinzie: Yerra, wasn't I only coddin' you. Put me up on your back, Jack, like a good boy.

Jack: Sure you won't flake me with the whip?

Dinzie: No fear, Jack. Is it me whip my own little pony? Come on now, Jack. Give us a hoist up.

(Reluctantly, wearily, Jack puts Dinzie up on his back. Dinzie cracks his whip)

Dinzie: D'you know what we'll have now, Jack. We'll have tables.

Jack: Tables, Dinzie?

Dinzie: Tables is right, Jack. Two and two is four. Tables, Jack. (*Contemplates*) We'll start with Miss Dee. (*To Miss Dee*) How much is the cost of seventeen quarts of porter, if blackberries were a guinea a bundle?

(Miss Dee frowns irritably)

> (*Clicking his tongue*) Should be four slaps by right, Jack, but we'll try her with another one. Hmmm! Let me see now ... how much is the price of nine canisters of nettles if hearts is trumps an' the ace is robbin'?

Miss Dee: Get away, you cheeky bla'guard!

Dinzie: She's very bad, Jack, very bad! Four slaps I'd say now!

Jack: Ah, can't you stop, Dinzie? If you don't be quiet now I'll put you down again.

Dinzie: (*Menace*) If you do, I'll choke you.

Jack: Ah, sure, I was only mockin', Dinzie.

Dinzie: I'll give her one more question and if she doesn't answer it I'll have to give her the slaps. Fair is fair, Jack. We can't have no favourites. Now, the last question. Supposin' you left water flowing into a bucket when would you have it filled? ... (*Waits for answer*) ... Ah, Jack, there's no meaning to this ...

(Dinzie suddenly leans sideways and gives Miss Dee a smack of the whip across the ankles. Miss Dee jumps up with a scream)

Miss Dee: Oh, you little hellion! I'll have the law on you! ...

(Miss Dee retreats backwards towards the kitchen)

Dinzie: After her, Jack! ... After her! ... After her, the wine-sucking gossiper!

(Dinzie makes several attempts to whip Miss Dee secondly but she runs into the kitchen. Dinzie guides Jack back triumphantly and confronts Moll and Mague)

Dinzie: Two lively scholars, here, Jack!

Jack: Ah, Dinzie, 'tisn't right. There'll be trouble. What will happen if Miss Dee goes for the guards?

Dinzie: She'd be afraid to go for the guards. Doesn't she know what'd befall her after. We won't be in jail for ever, Jack! Now, we'll test out the lassies here. (*He draws the whip downwards at the six women on the chairs*) Go on, ye thievin' hussies, gallivantin' around the country, spyin' on people an' back-lashin' and cutting.

(Dinzie whips the women into the kitchen. Neelus bolts out through the front door in terror. With the room empty, Dinzie raises the whip aloft)

Glory, Dinzie Conlee! Glory to the man who hunted the grabbers and snappers. Glory to his brother Jack who carried him up on his back. Glory to the bould Dinzie for a gaiscíoch and a hayro and may scabs and scour descend on all the vagabonds and villains that come to people's wakes to gossip and spy like beggars for whiskey and porter, for snuff and tobacco.

Jack: Ah, go aisy, Dinzie. Go aisy, let you!

(Dinzie gives Jack a vicious wallop in the back)

Jaminy, but you'll capsize me, Dinzie! You've hurted me, man!

Dinzie: Put me down Jack. Put me down 'till I get a rest after that. We cleared the room, Jack – Dinzie Conlee and his brother Jack. (*Jack puts Dinzie on the chair. Dinzie lifts the bottle and hands it to Jack*) Drink up, Jack. 'Tis great for the gizzard!

(Jack swallows heartily from the bottle and shakes his head after it. Jack might roll on floor and kick out like a horse, whinnying as he does)

Jack: 'Tis strong stuff!

Dinzie: Give us a song, Jack!

Jack: Ah, I wouldn't like to, Dinzie.

Dinzie: Glory to Jack Conlee, with the voice of a thrush.

Jack: (*Doubtfully*) Would it be any harm, do you think?

Dinzie: No harm at all. Won't it shorten the road for him? (*Indicates the corpse*)

Jack: Will I give 'The boys of Ned's mountain'? 'Tis an airy one.

(Jack assumes a singing stance and clears his throat. Enter Trassie. She glares at Dinzie)

Trassie: Are you going out of your mind ... what right have you to drive all these people out of the room? Whipping Miss Dee and the women the same as if they were cattle. How dare you do that in this house where you have no right.

Dinzie: No right! ... Isn't this my house now?

Trassie: It is not your house!

Dinzie: (*Shrilly, thumping the chair*) 'Tis my house! 'Tis my house! You'll be comin' over to our house when we bury what's in the bed.

Trassie: I'm going down to the kitchen to tell the people you're sorry – that you didn't know what you were doing, you were so foolish with the drink.

Dinzie: Tell them nothing, or I'll use the whip again. I'll mark 'em this time. I swear I'll mark 'em. I'll file the skin off their bones.

Trassie: (*Menace*) Dinzie Conlee, I'm going down into the kitchen now, and I'll be coming back to this room again in the space of a few minutes. If you aren't gone home, I'll call the dogs in from the yard.

Dinzie: Don't be upsetting me now! Don't be upsetting me. I have a plan in my head.

Trassie: A plan! ... What plan?

Dinzie: We'll have Neelus examined.

Trassie: Examined! ... By whom?

Dinzie: By the father of all doctors.

Trassie: He was examined before by doctors and they said there was nothing to be done. They said he was harmless.

Dinzie: (*Thumps the chair*) He isn't harmless, I tell you. Wait 'till he be examined by a proper doctor and we'll soon find out what's wrong with him.

Trassie: What are you talking about?

Dinzie: (*Pause*) Pats Bo Bwee!

Trassie: (*Wonder*) Pats Bo Bwee!

Dinzie: Pats Bo Bwee, the Cures, from the Wiry Glen. He has cures for all aches and pains, for every dizaze you could put a name to.

Trassie: He's not a doctor!

Dinzie: He's better than any doctor.

Trassie: He's a quack!

Dinzie: D'you hear that, Jack? D'you hear her? D'you hear what she is calling Pats Bo Bwee? A man that could read your mind for you? She's calling Pats Bo Bwee a quack? If he heard you he'd turn the eyes around in your head, and give you a dose of the itch.

Trassie: Maybe he has cures, but he's not a doctor.

Dinzie: He'd lose what doctors are in the country. There was an old man, blind, beyond Lenamore, that never saw the sight of day or night in twenty years. Pats Bo Bwee gave him a black bottle and a clatter into the side of the poll with his brass hammer and didn't the sight come back to him and he saw twice as much as he saw before.

Trassie: He knows nothing about Neelus.

Dinzie: What harm what harm, 'tis how you're afraid to bring him over. 'Tis how you're afraid of what he'll tell you, for you know well in your heart and soul that Neelus is as cracked as the crows and worse he's getting.

Trassie: I am not afraid. Why should I be afraid?

Dinzie: Pats Bo Bwee will put his finger on the harm. You know he will and you don't want Neelus' trouble to be known.

Trassie: I know what Neelus' trouble is.

Dinzie: Ah … but do you know what his trouble is? If you're so sure why won't you let him be examined?

Trassie: I'm not afraid to have Pats Bo Bwee see him. Why would I when I know that Neelus is as harmless as a child in the crib?

Dinzie: I'll have Pats Bo Bwee here the day after the funeral. I'll tell him to bring his brass hammer and his bag of cures. Thanking me you should be that I'm doing this for Neelus. Wait 'till Pats Bo Bwee is finished with him and you'll soon know what the trouble is ... Put me up on your back, Jack, and carry me home ... carry me home, Jack!

Jack: (*Helping Dinzie on to his back*) Get a good grip, Dinzie. (*Hoists him on his back*)

Dinzie: Don't be giving out wine and whiskey to them scroungers in the kitchen. That's all they're here for, for what they can get out of you. (*To Jack*) Go on, pony ... go on up, there. (*Hits Jack on the back*)

Jack: Didn't I tell you not to be calling me 'pony'. Do you want the people of Baltavinn to be calling me 'pony'.

Dinzie: Yerra, 'tisn't a pony you are at all, Jack, but a horse. Sure, you're desperate strong. Open the door and we'll be going ... I'll have Pats Bo Bwee over the day after tomorrow ... go on, Jack! Go on – are you going to keep me here all night?

(Jack opens the door and exits, with Dinzie on his back. When they have gone, Trassie tidies the room and collects a few discarded empty glasses from the floor. After a few moments the latch lifts and Peadar Minogue enters)

Trassie: Did you go a long ways on your walk?

Peadar: Just over the fields a piece, down to where there is the deep hole with the sea coming in under it – the hole they call Sharon's grave.

Trassie: That is a dangerous place! Many is the fine cow that fell into it, never again to be seen. You know the story?

Peadar: But that is a pagan story, surely, and not one you could believe.

Trassie: Oh, to be sure, it is a pagan story but the old people ... many of them believe it to be true.

Peadar: It was sad that Sharon should die in such a way.

Trassie: It is lonesome to think of her falling into the dark and sad to think of her young sweetheart waiting, never again to see her.

Peadar: Thinking about it would be lonesome.

Trassie: Sometimes when the moon is a full moon over the sea, Neelus will go down and sing lullabies for Sharon, thinking to give her sleep.

Peadar: No harm in it, surely, that he should want to help a soul in trouble.

Trassie: I shouldn't be talking like this with my father dead. Praying I should be!

Peadar: A thing to talk about is good. I saw your cousins from the fields. I could see the small fellow, on his brother's back. Like a horse and jockey they were. The two of them were singing to wake the country. (*Hesitantly*) Was there any trouble while I was out?

Trassie: Nothing to bother about.

Peadar: If there was trouble, I could help, maybe!

Trassie: (Looks at him as if she would tell, but changes her mind. They look at each other) How could you help and you next to nothing to me and it would be no way fair to expect you to interfere. People like you are kind but relatives are the very devil and a death in the house makes them ten times worse and turns life into a bedlam.

(Curtain)

ACT TWO
SCENE I

The action takes place in the kitchen of Trassie Conlee's farmhouse. The time is four days later, mid morning. Trassie is cutting seed potatoes at the table. She wears a sack over her skirt. She uses a common kitchen knife for the cutting. While she is thus occupied Peadar Minogue enters by the front door.

Trassie: What is the day doing?

Peadar: The day is holding up fine. There's a dry wind from the sea and there's no rain likely.

Trassie: Did you see Neelus?

Peadar: I saw him. He had the drills opened for the potatoes. He was starting to draw manure.

Trassie: 'Twould be an ease to get the potatoes down. We could begin with the bog then. We have three sleens of turf to cut and make up. I suppose you'll be going your road now?

Peadar: 'Tis time to go, I'd say! I am very thankful to you for keeping me these last days.

Trassie: 'Tis how I should be thanking you ... the great help you were to us.

Peadar: That was nothing.

Trassie: Will you go back to your brother's house now, or will you go north in search of work?

Peadar: I think I'll chance the north – the Kerry Head direction – cross over into Clare. There should be work.

Trassie: What kind is your own home in the mountains?

Peadar: Only a small place with the grass of a few cows.

Trassie: Is your brother the older of the two of you?

Peadar: No, I'm a year older. My mother died after he was born.

Trassie: God rest her! ... Shouldn't the place be yours, though, if you are the eldest?

Peadar: It was willed to me by my father.

Trassie: And how is it, then, that your brother has it?

Peadar: He married a girl he was fond of and he had no place to take her, so I gave the place over to him.

Trassie: And did you not think to marry yourself?

Peadar: I thought about it often enough but there was no one I was fond of.

Trassie: (*Pause*) Wasn't it foolish to give away your house and land and cattle?

Peadar: There is always a place for me there. My brother is a good brother and his wife is a kindly person.

Trassie: Would you think of working at anything else besides the thatching?

Peadar: I am best at the thatching, but I wouldn't turn away from a day's work of any kind.

Trassie: There is work here for a few weeks, maybe longer, if you like to stay. We would pay what we could.

Peadar: There is no need for payment. I would be very happy to work here for my keep.

Trassie: Why is that?

Peadar: (*Awkwardly*) It is a nice place to be.

Trassie: There will be hard work in the bog, and then there are the crops and the corn.

Peadar: No matter! I'll get used to it.

Trassie: What do they call the place you come from?

Peadar: Glashnanaon.

Trassie: That's a nice name – Glashnanaon!

Peadar: 'The stream of the birds'!

Trassie: I know! Are there many birds there, then?

Peadar: It is a great place for linnets. And you could hardly count the swarms of finches. 'Tis the first place you'll hear the cuckoo and come the winter the pilibíns fill the sky with their call so that, all in all, winter or summer, we have our fair share of birdsong.

Trassie: All you will hear in these parts is the seagull or maybe the curlew crying in the rain when 'tis dark and stormy. The curlew crying is lonely but it is nice to hear when you have a good bed to sleep in.

Peadar: Maybe you will come visiting some time to my brother's house in Glashnanaon. You could bring Neelus. He would like to see the finches.

Trassie: Maybe some day when the weather is fine we would go visiting. It is nice, too, here in Carraig Head in the height of summer. You can sit on the trippols of finnaun over the cliff and you would see the ships passing down the coast, little ships only.

Peadar: I imagine it would be nice of a fine day to sit and watch the ships passing. I hope there will be work enough to keep me through the summer. It would be nice.

Trassie: Maybe there will. We have three mountain meadows that have to be cut with a scythe. Plenty work in that. 'Tis settled then that you'll stay for a tamaill?

Peadar: If you want me.

Trassie: It would be good to have you. There is money to be made in the pooleens of the stream that flows near the meadows. A man with a good net and a head on his shoulders wouldn't want for salmon. They fetch a fair price in Lenamore in the summer.

Peadar: It wouldn't be my first time poaching salmon. Of course, a man alone ... (*shrugs*)

Trassie: Neelus is afraid of the pooleens but I have an eye for bailiffs as good as any man when the salmon are there.

(*There is a knock at the door, a long steady knock*)

Who could that be, at this early hour of the day?

Peadar: Maybe Dinzie Conlee and his brother.

Trassie: They would never knock.

Peadar: Who, then?

Trassie: Maybe a tinker man looking for the colouring of his tea or a stranger enquiring his way. You would never know at this time of day. (*She moves towards the door and calls*) Who is it that's out?

Voice: (*Thunderous, yet refined, of most musical south-western tone*) Pats Bo Bwee with his bag on his back. Pats Bo Bwee, from the Wiry Glen.

Trassie: (*Excitedly*) Pats Bo Bwee! Oh! Dia Linn! Looking for Neelus he is.

Peadar: I heard tell of Pats Bo Bwee. That's the man with the great name out of him for cures.

(Trassie, flustered, opens the door. Enter Pats Bo Bwee. He is sixtyish, florid, bearded, with a great advance-guard of a stomach. He carries his leonine head thrown back. He wears a small coat tightly buttoned over his protuberance of stomach. He carries a bag on his back. He wears an ancient hat with a large quivering feather. He wears corduroy trousers, hob-nailed boots and shirt open at the neck. He gives the impression of health and vigour belying his years. He surveys the kitchen indulgently)

Pats: The last time I put my foot inside this door was twenty-seven years ago. Kawtee Conlee, your grandmother, was alive at the time. She was suffering from 'the runs'. It nearly killed her, but I cured her. 'Tis four walking miles from the Wiry Glen to Baltavinn and four more back.

Trassie: *(Arranges a chair for him)* Will you sit down, and I will make tea for you? *(Anxiously)*

Pats: It was a great sorrow with me that I wasn't here for your father's wake. I was beyond in Glounsharoon attending to the father of nine children. He got a swelling on his elbow and I gave the best part of a week curing him. By all ac-counts it was a wake to be remembered! I drinks tea but sel-dom. There is great boasting in Baltavinn about the whiskey that was brought to this house. A man was heard to say that 'twould take a week to drink it.

Trassie: There's whiskey left if you care for it. I should have asked you in the first place. You'll think very poorly

75

of us in Baltavinn, the small respect we show you ... I won't be long.

(Exit Trassie. Pats Bo Bwee goes and sits on the chair previously proffered by Trassie. He places his bag between his legs and his stick across his knee)

Pats: What name have they for you?

Peadar: My name is Peadar Minogue.

Pats: What keeps you here?

Peadar: There was a death ...

Pats: What is death but a long rest beyond the door and no more! What is death but a slipping away till we gather again.

(Peadar makes no answer but walks a little to and fro)

   (*Authoritatively, pompous*) You say your name is Peadar Minogue. I say my name is Pats Bo Bwee. I am Pats Bo Bwee with my one yalla cow and my cures. But who are you?

Peadar: I'm Peadar Minogue, the thatcher.

Pats: (*Stamps foot*) But what keeps you here?

Peadar: I stay here only for Trassie Conlee.

Pats: And you tell me you stay here only for Trassie Conlee! Do you ever get pains?

Peadar: No pain yet. I thank God for that.

Pats: Where is the boy of the house?

Peadar: There are no boys here, or girls either – only two men and the one woman.

Pats: I'm cursed with the flowers of genius. I'm danged from thinking nether thoughts. I'm wore, wore to the bone thatch-er. Now where is Neelus Conlee that's gone simple?

Peadar: Neelus Conlee is out working his day's work.

Pats: When is he due to arrive?

Peadar: For his dinner.

Pats: Is there meat for the dinner?

Peadar: I couldn't tell you that. I'm not boiling it.

Pats: You'll be eating it.

Peadar: What's boiled must be eat.

Pats: What's boiled must be eat indeed. Otherwise why boil! (*Winningly, to Peadar*) What time is dinner?

Peadar: It changes, day in, day out. Noon one day. Evening the next. One should wait for the call.

Pats: Did you travel, thatcher?

Peadar: Some!

Pats: Ah, but did you travel the mind? ... We were all at Aonachmore at the pattern and there's more went to America, but did you travel the mind ... strange roads in that country, thatcher!

(Enter Trassie, with two glasses in her hand, one filled with whiskey and the other partly filled. She hands the small quantity to Peadar and the large one to Pats Bo Bwee, who accepts the large as his due)

    (Toasts) God increase wakes. *(Taking a goodly swallow of whiskey – toasts)* That we may never lose the tooth for it! *(Swallows his drink in a gulp)*

Trassie: *(Taking glass)* Would you have more of it?

Pats: Enough is enough! We mustn't make pigs of ourselves. 'Twould be as well to bring in the boy of the house. I have a call to make in Goildarrig to a stutterin' child and I have a woman calling to the Wiry Glen tonight with blisters on her behind. There's a heifer calf in Trieneragh with the white scour – all waiting to be cured.

Trassie: Was it Dinzie Conlee told you to call?

Pats: *(Surprised only slightly)* He told me that young Neelus Conlee was ailing with a troubled head. It should be aisy to cure for there is no dúchas. I never heard of a Conlee being soft in the head.

Trassie: There is nothing much the matter with Neelus.

There were two doctors from Lenamore with him and they said he would always be the same. They said he would never be violent but that he was finished with words of sense.

Pats: (*Uplifts his head*) Doctors must account for their aisy lives. They always have some story for you. Mind you, I don't condemn. We must be on the one word. You'll never hear of a thrush eating another thrush.

Trassie: Peadar, will you call Neelus in from the fields.

Peadar: (*Putting his glass on the table*) I'll call him in.

Pats: (*Uplifts his head*) I'll call out and call him in! (*Rises pompously. Points at the bag*) The curse of the crows on the hands that interfere with the work of Pats Bo Bwee or goes near his bag.

Trassie: What harm would it do if some one else called him?

Pats: Did you not ever hear of the devils in hell? The way they do have their ears cocked? Do ye know the misfortune that might befall your brother if one of ye called him? There's no devils at all in hell except a few tending their fires. The rest of 'em, to be around tormentin' people and coaxin' them and working their best plans to fool them. (Dramatic pause) God forbid that Pats Bo Bwee would ever say a word against the devils. We all have our faults and 'tis as well to be in with the two sides. 'Tis only a brave man like myself that would open his mouth against either of the two, with the grave staring me in the face.

Trassie: Let you call him yourself, so. Far be it from me to go putting obstacles in your way.

(Pats Bo Bwee goes to the front door, opens it and looks out, standing with great dignity – stomach protruding)

Pats: Let ye put no hands to my bag or be for feeling it to find what's inside fearin' ye might come to harm.

(Exit Pats Bo Bwee. After he has gone Trassie resumes her seed-cutting, slowly, abstractly. Peadar walks nearer to her)

Peadar: Trassie!

Trassie: (*Startled*) What is it?

Peadar: Do you think that this Pats Bo Bwee or what's in his bag will cure a person or ease a troubled person? What I mean is that Neelus is what he is, 'tis delicate, the handling. A man should want to know him well.

Trassie: There is a great name out of him for curing.

Peadar: It could be – but who is to cure a troubled mind?

Trassie: There is no harm in attempting it. I know, as well as I know my own hands, that Neelus is harmless.

Peadar: Why so do you allow Pats Bo Bwee to examine him? Why should you let a man like that decide what thing is before your brother?

Trassie: Because I know there is nothing up with Neelus.

Peadar: (*Deliberate tone*) I will be leaving Baltavinn tomorrow or the day after.

Trassie: I thought to hear you say you would be staying a while.

Peadar: I don't hold with what's going on! I don't hold with Bo Bwee or your cousins Dinzie and Jack Conlee.

Trassie: I am doing the best thing I know.

Peadar: There is nothing in the oul' bag except maybe bottles of water or cut rushes.

Trassie: They say he has great powers and by all accounts there's a bad curse out of him.

Peadar: If he is so wise why is it he is the way he is? Why should he be so full of draoidheacht and mystery instead of saying his say openly. An honest man will give you his whole mind.

Trassie: (*Hurriedly*) You never gave your whole mind. How is one to know what's in a person's mind, anyway?

Peadar: How do you mean?

Trassie: How do I mean, only that you were a stranger first and now I don't know what you are for sure.

Peadar: (*Embarrassed, puzzled*) Just that I was a bit bothered about ye.

Trassie: Why should you be bothered about Neelus or about the cures of Pats Bo Bwee? (*Hurriedly*) Why should you be troubled about the way things are in this house or why should you trouble yourself to stay at all when you are so well used to the roads? Or what private thing of your own keeps you under the one roof so long? (*She cuts the seed quickly*)

Peadar: I stay here ... (*Looks away*) ... I stay here because you were pleasant and not full of pride when I first put my foot inside your door.

Trassie: Was that what brought you then, the chance of a bed with sheets, and the chance of keeping your feet under a table three times a day with no worry of the roads before you?

Peadar: I was hungry often and many a night without a bed but many a man without a home to go to will find himself in the same tangle of trouble. It's nothing to a single man who has no one to worry about him.

Trassie: You have a free life. Fine for you to be so.

Peadar: I travelled every road of the west coast but I never gave more than two nights under a roof in the same house. The urge not to remain was in me. I have given the best part of a week here, what I have never done.

Trassie: (*Charmingly*) Why do you give so much time here?

Peadar: (*Pause*) You!

(*Peadar turns to examine the wall at the rear. Trassie stands stock-still*)

Trassie: It's time I looked after the dinner.

Peadar: It's early yet.

(*Trassie is about to return to the table to continue to cut the potatoes*)

Peadar: (*Throatily*) There is a pile of things I could tell you, if you let me.

Trassie: What things?

Peadar: (*Turning, uncertain tone*) I would say you are among the best girls I have seen upon my rounds.

Trassie: Go on with you!

Peadar: I would say things all day to you.

Trassie: (*Without rising her head*) What things?

Peadar: I would say that you have eyes in your head like a stormy evening; that you have calves to your legs like a pair of running trout; that you have a voice that would keep a man awake at night thinking, and, above all things, that you would be a lovely person to have near-abouts to be telling things to. I would say I would like to have soft hold of your two hands.

Trassie: You would say that.

Peadar: I would say that. I would say likewise that I would love to sit and watch you at your work. I would love to see you moving here and there and be watching and admiring you. I would think things then to myself about you.

Trassie: What things?

Peadar: Things, maybe, you would not like.

Trassie: Only a miser would keep a nice thought.

Peadar: If you want to hear, so here it is. (*Bends head*) I would think of the beauty of you, of the way your eyes do be, and how I would give my heart and soul to be lying down in your bed and to be holding you and feeling your softness against me. It is too sweet and hurtful to think of it. To think of the lovely body under your clothes, and to think of the wintry nights when I would be shielding the soft trembling white-ness of you from the cold and we whispering together in a room with nobody else in it.

Trassie: You should not say that!

Peadar: I am a man, amn't I? ... You are a girl of rare niceness with pretty ways to you and a neat form by you. If I said another thing I would be telling lies. I have a terrible longing for you, growing worse lately, growing worse every time you will look my way.

Trassie: It is wrong of you to be saying this with my father only barely buried.

Peadar: (*Angrily*) The dead are dead and won't they be always dead. Will you have them rise up again out of their graves and be changing the pattern of things that are alive and with us. (*Gently*) I'm sorry, Trassie, to give you hurt. I know the feelings you store for your dead father and I am weak for your sorrow. (*Dramatic pause – Peadar is in real anger – violent anger*) But I swear by the Lord God that made me, I will have the life of Dinzie Conlee if he comes here again before I leave; if he comes here again frightening you. I've seen the look of worry and fear in your eyes when they're here. (*Angrily*) I will let no man frighten you!

Trassie: 'Tis temper now!

Peadar: (*Calmly, slowly*) Temper is what it is! What else would I have except it was temper. I will! ... I will! And I swear this by the mother of God ... I will tear the heart out of Jack Conlee, your cousin, if he lays a hand on you. (*Uplifts his finger*) I will! ... I warn you! ... I will take the life blood from the two of them if they make a fool of your brother Neelus. It was not my place here to interfere but there is too much of thievery going on and I will not sing dumb when I see it.

Trassie: I never thought to see such a temper in you! You're like a devil with temper.

Peadar: (*With humour*) I'm worse than a devil. I'm a man.

Trassie: (*Gently, seriously*) I would not like to tease you, Peadar.

(Peadar goes and takes Trassie's hands suddenly in his, holding them roughly)

Peadar: Now I have your hands and, God forgive me for a coward, I haven't the courage to see what's in your eyes.

(He lets go of her hands and looks directly at her. Trassie closes her eyes, Peadar places his hands over them and he takes her face in his hands. She opens her eyes, and smiles at him)

Now I have your head in my hands and your lovely face under my fingers, and I have to feel you ... I have to feel you for the ease of my body and my mind. I have to feel your kind back within my hands and your lively breasts to my chest. I have to feel the ease of the woman that you are against me. (*She yields wholly to his embrace*) I have to hold you against me for I keep the picture of what is happening now with me. It is joy to hold you, Trassie – pure joy!

Trassie: (*Whispers*) Peadar!

(Peadar holds her tightly and kisses her face and, finally, her lips. The door opens and Neelus enters. He looks stupidly at Trassie and Peadar, who break apart. Trassie resumes her work and Peadar stands to one side. Neelus is followed by Pats Bo Bwee)

Pats: M'anam an diabhail, but this is a great wall of an idiot. Four times I called him and four times he hung his head. 'Come up here, you gamalóg!' says I for a finish, but there wasn't a hum or a haw out of him, so I caught him by the sleeve of his coat and brought him here. Does he be like this always?

Trassie: There is no harm in him.

Pats: Doesn't he know I have people to cure in other parts. You will have to give me the use of the table there.

(Trassie gathers the potatoes into a pot. Peadar turns to watch. Pats Bo Bwee takes his bag and with ceremony places it on the table. He directs Neelus to sit on a chair. Neelus sits in a frightened way)

Trassie: This is Pats Bo Bwee from the Wiry Glen, Neelus. He is only trying to help you.

Pats: He has the wild eyes of his grandfather.

Peadar: What will you do for him?

Pats: *(To the ceiling – pompously)* Ye will all leave the kitchen now, a-barring myself and the boy. Too many times rogues and scoundrels have stolen my cures and made fortunes for themselves.

Peadar: What would I want with your oul' cures?

Pats: Every spailpín in the country is aching for the knowledge I contain, and when they can't have it they will have curses pouring down on the top of me ... (*Magnanimously*) What harm, if it will make them content. I bear no hate ... (*Distantly, slightly reproving*) Ye will leave now! I have work before me. This is no place for common people.

(Trassie takes Peadar by the hand and leads him through the side exit. He follows grudgingly)

Pats: Hide nothing from me, gearrcach. I have seen the minds of people like you before. The priest hearing sin in his box will forgive what he's told, but Pats Bo Bwee will find out hidden things.

(Pats opens his bag delicately and produces a hammer with a head of brass. The head is highly burnished, the handle delicate and of tiny circumference. Pats lays the hammer on the table and explores further into the bag. He produces several stalks of mature rag-wort and lays them on the table. He produces a number of egg-shells, cup-shape as if the shells were neatly divided (these would be for measures of medicines). He lays several of these on the table together with a handled clay container, gallon size, which he shakes and holds to his ear. Satisfied, he places the container on the table and takes his brass hammer in hand. He passes in front of Neelus and takes his stand at his side. He holds the hammer behind his back and surveys Neelus professionally)

Pats: Is it women that's troubling you, or is it the stars? (*Neelus looks frightened*) I think a tip of the hammer is what you want.

(Ceremoniously he brings the hammer to the front, fondles it and suddenly taps Neelus on the head, with some force. He leans forward eagerly)

Did you feel that? Did you feel as if someone spoke to you? *(Neelus looks at him)* Out with it!

Neelus: *(Hesitant)* I remember to hear my father talking when I was small.

Pats: Aaah! ... you did, did you! So well you might, you mad scut! So well you might, what more?

Neelus: *(With some ray of understanding)* I remember the bed, with my mother, and to see my father shaving and to be watching him. (Neelus pauses, dejectedly), and to be playing with Trassie in the meadows (Absently, lovingly). And Trassie taking me by the hand to school and I remember Trassie with her white dress at confirmation. Trassie was sweet.

Pats: Go on! Go on, you folbo! Tell!

(Enter Peadar angrily with Trassie clutching his hand. Peadar pauses and he hears Neelus)

Neelus: *(Rubs his head)* I remember my father ... to sit in his lap ... *(Wanderingly, truthfully)* To sit on his lap and be warm, secure, like the pony in the stable ... and to watch him smoking his pipe and he looking at me, laughing. They were all outside my father's lap. They were all outside. I saw the entire lot looking in at me and they watching my father ... my father ... (*Loneliness, abject*) ... my father and he lifting me up into the air ... the strength of my father ... (*Pathetically*) ... Dada! Dada!

(Pats taps Neelus viciously with the hammer)

Pats: Dada! Dada! Is your head that empty? When your father was buried you were laughing and talking to yourself or so the countryside says. Is your memory as short or is it going altogether?

Neelus: (*Childishly – to impress Pats. Tone of awe*) The rain is belting the black rocks and the white horses are rearing in the sea. Sharon is olagóning in her grave and Shíofra is screeching in the belly of the wind.

Pats: (*Stands back in amazement*) Oh, Lord God in your fine house above us with angels and saints attending to you, give me patience with this fool – who is seven different kinds of a fool. Come away from your angels and saints and give ear to the words of Pats Bo Bwee and tell me not to tamper with the mind of this bollav.

Peadar: Leave Neelus alone!

Pats: He is to be examined, and he will be examined. No man interferes with Pats Bo Bwee.

Trassie: (*Fearfully*) It might be better to leave him alone, Peadar.

Pats: (*To Neelus*) We will go up to the room and bolt the door and I will work my cures in peace.

Peadar: (*Snatches the hammer from Pat's hand*) You will work your cures without this.

Pats: (*Draws himself to his full height*) I will work my cures with nothing at all. (*To Neelus*) Up to the room!

(Neelus rises and goes to the room quietly, followed by Pats Bo Bwee who turns and looks at Peadar)

Minogue, from the bogholes of Glashnanaon, put my ham-mer from you or your hand will waste. They say that Glashnanaon is a hive of thieves. They say that if a man stuck out his tongue there 'twould be stolen off him by the thieving tricksters of Glashnanaon.

(Pats Bo Bwee turns and exits the room after Neelus. Peadar throws the hammer on to the table in disgust)

Peadar: Trassie, there is no meaning to having that man in the house. You know as well as I do that he is as false as a boghole. You know well that he was sent here by Dinzie Conlee and that he was paid money by Dinzie Conlee to come here.

Trassie: Everyone sends for Pats Bo Bwee when all fruit fails.

Peadar: Are you so much afraid of Dinzie Conlee, Trassie?

Trassie: Dinzie is dangerous! Jack is bad but you could fight with Jack and you could beat him but you couldn't beat Dinzie. Not Dinzie. Nobody could get the better of Dinzie Conlee.

Peadar: I see nothing to fear in either of the pair of them.

Trassie: You don't know Dinzie, Peadar. Dinzie would do for you. Do you know he carries a long knife with him in hide where no one can see it? He can be sweet, too. He'd let on to be all about you and that's the time you couldn't trust him at all.

Peadar: I wouldn't fear him. I'd watch him.

Trassie: No! No! Leave Dinzie alone! He's madder than anything in this world. He has no faith in anything. You couldn't trick with Dinzie. He might be doing one thing but he would still be watching all things. You'll never know what he's watching or what he's thinking.

(Enter Pats Bo Bwee, triumphant – pushing a dejected Neelus in front of him)

Pats: (*In a rage – throws his hands. To Neelus*) There's a devil in you! Clear out, you devil you! The devil is 'ating away at your mind and sould and you're clear and clane mad altogether. There is no cure for you that grows in the ground. God give me a silver bed in heaven for the patience I have with you.

(Frightened, Neelus flies before Pats' fury. Pats stands in the doorway calling)

> Go on! Gallop away like the mountainy jackass that you are. Gallop away from the sight and sound of God-fearing people. Gallop away into the wind and the wild air where demons are dwelling and sweeping around the bare windy roads of the sky! ... Go! ... Go!

Trassie: Is something wrong? What's wrong with him? Where is he going? *(Innocently)* Did you send him on a journey?

(Dignified, Pats returns his cures to his bag, takes his stick in hand and slings his bag over his shoulder. He stands up with great hauteur)

Pats: I will cure warts, boils and carbuncles. I will put hair growing on a man's palm. I'll put a woman by way of having a child and I'll knit broken bones *(Loudly)*, but I vow! I vow to you, that I will have no truck with geowckacks.

Trassie: Geowckacks!

Pats: Geowckacks and fostooks like that savage of a brother you have, that would take my sacred life but for that he was afraid of my brassy hammer.

Peadar: Your brassy hammer is on the table!

(Pats quickly accepts the hammer and conceals same on his person)

Pats: Where is he, you say? ... (*Points stick at door*) Where is he but gone as fast as his legs will take him to the gravelly slopes of the moon.

Trassie: But why ... ?

Pats: (*Pointing his stick upwards*) Because he's mad! ... Mad! ... Mad! (*He opens door*) He's as mad as a flea on a hot coal. I'll have no handling of him. He's as mad as the heidle fo peeb and the heidle fo peeb is as mad as the breeze. Dinzie Conlee instructed me well. Dinzie Conlee said he was mad all along. I should have taken the advice of sensible people and stayed away from this house where a common thatcher is the master. (*Exit Pats Bo Bwee with dignity, closing the door behind him – Trassie stands a moment and then resumes her preparation for the dinner but then withdraws dejectedly from the table and sits on the chair nearest her and buries her face in her hands and is seen to be crying – Peadar stands idly, helplessly, watching her*)

(*Curtain*)

ACT TWO
SCENE II

The action takes place in the kitchen as before. The time is a day later.
It is evening.

> *Trassie sits near the window, patching the sleeve of an old coat.*
> *While she is thus engaged Neelus enters. He sits on a chair near the*
> *table, clasping and unclasping his hands, despondently.*

> *Trassie peers at him carefully.*

Trassie: Where is Peadar?

Neelus: You does be kissing with him and he does be holding
you. (*Trassie holds her breath*) There is a storm outside,
Trassie, I see the two of ye holding together the day
of Pats Bo Bwee.

Trassie: (*Nervously*) You did not!

Neelus: I see him with his hands around you, givin' kisses on
to you.

Trassie: What harm is there in kissing or holding?

Neelus: (*Tearfully*) I have no girl. I have only Sharon below in
her grave and she crying the whole time and Shíofra
do be scolding her.

Trassie: That is only an old bit of gossip for ageing people.
Why do you be going down there at night like an old
fool, singing to them, leaving your warm bed behind

you? ... The day we take the calves to town, I will buy you a Jew's harp.

Neelus: And ... a red concertina with a yellow belly?

Trassie: I will buy that same.

Neelus: And a fiddle and a German flute for me too?

Trassie: A fiddle and a German flute for sure and certain, the day we sell the calves.

Neelus: (*Somewhat appeased*) What else will you buy for me?

Trassie: (*Motherly tone*) Oh, I will buy you an aghaidh-fidil for the Wren's day at the year end. (Stops sewing and looks upwards) I will buy you a gansey coloured yellow and green with white cuffs and I will buy you books with pictures of ships in them and black shiny shoes with buckles on.

Neelus: (*Childish, serious*) Did Sharon wear black, shiny shoes, Trassie?

Trassie: (*Reproach, mild*) Sharon is part of your head, Neelus!

Neelus: What else will you buy for me?

Trassie: (*Dreamily*) Oh ... I will buy currant-tops that you like and a white collar for your stripey shirt and maybe a hat for you going to Mass and maybe togs for bathing, and we could go down to the tide, Peadar and myself and yourself.

Neelus: (*Shakes his head in wonder*) Did Sharon have a hat on her head, Trassie? (*Looks up dreamily*) Or was it a ribbon she wore or a comb to gather the length of her golden hair. What was it she wore, Trass?

Trassie: Who's to know what she wore, Neelus, since 'tis years since she was drowned. Sure, nobody would take notice of Shíofra or Sharon or how is one to know they were there at all?

Neelus: (*Mysteriously, confidentially*) They were there all right, Trass. I does often hear them when you does all be in bed. (*Wonder and fright mingled*) Well, if you hear poor lovely little Sharon and she is giving sighs and sobs to the wind and her tears to the tide (*Then hatefully*) and that other little thing, that Shíofra, is never done with screeching back at the wind, out of temper, Trassie.

Trassie: (*Resumes her stitching*) You were very good, Neelus at our poor dada's funeral ... (*Pauses*) ... the mud on his boots and the sigh of him when he bended to take them off – my father. (*Sighs*) The stories he used to tell us. (Smiles sadly) The gay stories about cats that wore waistcoats and bon-hams that wouldn't eat their dinner unless they were dressed in collars and ties and the crows that used to go to their own schools the same as ours.

Neelus: (*Clasping and unclasping hands*) Poor dada ... poor dada ... every small bird I see on a tree or hopping, I think to myself of my poor dead dada.

(Enter Peadar Minogue)

Peadar: There's a desperate storm rising on all sides. 'Twill make a wild night. I wouldn't wish to be in a boat on the sea tonight.

Trassie: The clouds were flying across the sky all day – always the sign of a storm.

Neelus: Wait until you hear the wind tonight!

Peadar: Awful screeching like the inside of a pig's bladder if you blew it up and left it off. The Goureen Roe was calling for the rain in the bog.

Trassie: What about the sheep?

Peadar: I counted them all near the house. They're safe enough. They know the storm is breaking. Sheep aren't as foolish as people think.

Trassie: *(Putting the coat aside – rises)* Will we have a game of cards to pass the long evening?

Peadar: 'Twould give us something to do. What games do ye play in Baltavinn?

Trassie: 'Beggar thy neighbour' or 'A hundred and ten'. I'll get the deck in the room.

(Exit Trassie)

Neelus: I see you with your hands around Trassie.

Peadar: I am very fond of her.

Neelus: Why are you fond of her?

Peadar: I don't know why.

Neelus: Is she fond of you?

Peadar: I hope so, Neelus. I think, maybe. She might be a little bit fond of me. I hope she is.

Neelus: (*Mournfully*) I have no one that's fond of me!

Peadar: Trassie is fond of you, man; and I'm fond of you.

Neelus: Dinzie Conlee isn't fond of me!

(Enter Trassie with a pack of cards)

Trassie: We will play 'a hundred and ten'. Neelus can deal.

(They draw chairs to the table. Neelus sits at the head, Trassie at centre and Peadar at the bottom. Neelus deals three hands of five cards each and five to the side. They examine their cards)

Neelus: We will play for pennies. I'll chance twenty.

Trassie: I pass!

Peadar: I'll pass too

(Neelus takes the five other cards quickly and examines them and throws them down again)

Trassie: 'Tis hard to beat Neelus at 'a hundred and ten'. He has a great brain for following cards.

(Neelus deals cards secondly to Trassie and Peadar, but drops the

cards halfway through and sits bolt upright)

Trassie: What's wrong, Neelus?

(Neelus does not answer but sits listening. Trassie looks at Peadar)

Peadar: What's wrong, Neelus?

Neelus: It's them!

Peadar: Them! Who?

Neelus: 'Tis Dinzie and Jack, I hear Jack's feet.

Trassie: Oh, merciful God! And we having such peace.

(The three sit silently watching the door. Jack and Dinzie can be heard to approach. The door opens and Jack enters carrying Dinzie on his back)

Jack: Will I put you down, Dinzie?

Dinzie: (*Thumps Jack into back*) Aren't you in a great hurry with the poor oul' cripple. Set back a bit, let you, 'till we see what's here. Go back, pony ... back, boy ... back! (*Dinzie forces Jack to retreat while he surveys the occupants of the kitchen*) D'you see them, Jack? ... Ah, Jack, will you have a look at the faces of the craturs. Wouldn't you love to be like them? (*Loudly – pompously*) There should be no gambling allowed where there was death! 'Tis flying in the face of God. 'Tis the end of the world when people show no respect for the dead. Ye should be ashamed of yeer lives – gambling and arguing and cursing over money with yeer father roasting below in the halls of hell. Ye'll have no luck for it.

Jack: Will I put you down, Dinzie?

Dinzie: Will you go aisy! You're like an oul' woman, grumbling.

Jack: (*Wearily, first trace of anger*) Amn't I after galloping to the Wiry Glen today to see Pats Bo Bwee, and in to the town of Lenamore to Macky Flynn, the motor, and amn't I after coming here on top of it. You give me no peace or ease.

Dinzie: (*To trio*) Do you know at all what I'm going to do to Jack? I'm going to buy a pony's harness with bells on it for him and a reins made out of light leather and I'll make silver shoes for his feet.

(Dinzie gives Jack a thump in the small of the back. Jack winces and sets Dinzie down on a chair. Jack goes to the corner and begins to limber up and exercise his cramped muscles. He does this exaggeratedly. Then he takes off his coat and cap and helps Dinzie off with his. He goes through his exercises on floor)

Dinzie: (*Perched on the chair*) Ye'll be ready in the morning, Trassie.

(All watch him)

Trassie: Ready for what?

Dinzie: (*Vicious*) Ready to put your feet under you and leave here!

Trassie: Are you mad?

Dinzie: Not mad but in earnest! Today, myself and Jack walked all the ways to the town of Lenamore. We were telling the civic guards about Neelus and they said 'twould be safer to have him locked away.

Trassie: (*Rises*) What lies did you tell the civic guards?

Dinzie: I told what was true.

Trassie: You told lies, I know.

(*Peadar rises and glowers at Dinzie*)

Peadar: Better to take no notice of him Trassie.

(*Dinzie fumes and thumps his chair*)

Dinzie: (*Hysterically*) Listen to the lying tramp of a thatcher. Put me up on your back, Jack, 'till we kick the stomach out of him. Put me up, Jack, and we'll dance on his guts.

(*Jack goes to Dinzie's side. Peadar advances a step, fists clenched*)

Trassie: (*Command*) Peadar! (*Peadar stops*) Go out, to the stall and see if the cows are all right, and pacify the pony. He's afraid of storms.

(*Peadar looks at her doubtfully, and looks at Dinzie again, clenching his fists*)

Peadar: What about him?

Trassie: Go out now, Peadar, I'll be all right. I'll call if I want you.

(Peadar exits casting threatening looks at Jack and Dinzie)

Dinzie: That's right! Take the side of wandering villains that would murder you in your sleep.

(Dinzie scowls at Neelus. Neelus rises, looks fearfully at Dinzie, and exits)

Trassie: Why do you be always putting the heart crossways in Neelus when he has never done anything to you?

Dinzie: Because he's a blasted nuisance that should be under lock and key. We were at the Wiry Glen this morning, myself and Jack. Isn't that right, Jack?

Jack: That's right, Dinzie.

Dinzie: We were talking to Pats Bo Bwee and he's not feeling well, the poor man, after his visit to this house. He swore on his oath that Neelus will smother us all some night in our sleep. He swore on his oath that there's no madder amadán of a man from here to Donegal. Isn't that right, Jack?

Jack: He said it, all right, Trassie.

Trassie: And how much money did you give him?

Dinzie: *(Mystified)* Money! What money? Give him money for what? Explain to me, Jack, what she's saying. I never gave him money. That I might be as dead as my auntie Noney that's in her grave and my uncle Pat that was slaughtered by the turkeys in Salonika if I gave him money. Money for what?

Trassie: How much did you pay Pats Bo Bwee for saying Neelus was dangerous?

Dinzie: (*Puzzled*) What ails her, Jack, what ails her now? Sure she don't know what she's saying at all, Jack. God forgive her, she's getting wilent. 'Tis that rat's spawn of a thatcher that has this house upset. A man told me in a public house in Lenamore that you couldn't be up to the Minogues – that they were the greatest tribe of pratey-snapping mongrels from Goilldearg to the salt water.

Trassie: Go home, Dinzie. Take him home, Jack. He has no business here.

Dinzie: (*Thumps chair*) That's the respect she has for her uncle's son, her own flesh and blood, that's for her good.

Trassie: (*Firmly*) Dinzie Conlee, you're going out of this house now and you'll never come inside the door of it again. Take him up, Jack, and carry him away.

Dinzie: (*Thumps the chair, shouts*) I will not leave here! I will never leave here! My place is here! I want a little woman of my own to marry here! No one will have me if I haven't a house and land. What would you do if you had this millstone of mine on your back?

What would you do if you had only dead branches of legs? What would you do if you were never to feel the grassy ground under your feet or never to vault a gate or a ditch and you passing through land? What would you do when the fiddles are tuning up for the sets and everyone tapping toes on the stone floor? What would you do when the lads are kicking ball and you have a wild feeling to draw a kick for devilment? What would you do?

Trassie: 'Tis hard for you, I know, but it is no fault of mine. Go away from here – home!

Dinzie: (*Bitterly*) Aisy for you and for Jack here with yeer legs firm and strong and yeer straight backs. (*Shrieks*) I have nothing at all to show for myself. I have twists and turns to my body like a thorn tree. (*Roars*) I'm no fool! Dinzie Conlee's no fool. I know my value but if I have this place I will have plenty single women thinking of settling with me. (*Pleading*) Will you condemn me for that, Trassie? ... For thinking the way I do? (*Pause*) Everybody knows you yourself would have no trouble latching a man to you and I swear to God I will give you what few pounds I have to add to your fortune if you let me have this house. (*Pause*) ... And a bit o' land ... (*Pause*) ... and the few cows ... and the pony. (*Placatingly*) Won't we go visiting Neelus in his fine tall home when we get the fine day ... and the roads dry?

Trassie: (*Sincerely*) 'Tis a pity for you, but ... I have doubts about you – the way you made plans for Neelus as if he was mad.

Dinzie: (*Reverting to old, demoniacal self*) He is mad, I tell you! He's stone mad!

Trassie: How do you know but maybe 'tis yourself that's mad?

Dinzie: (*Thumps chair*) In what way would I be mad when I'm as sane as a man of ninety? Sure, you never heard anyone saying that I was mad.

Trassie: They be afraid to say it – afraid of yourself and Jack.

Dinzie: D'you hear that, Jack? Good almighty God, Jack, I say, did you hear that? I say, Jack, that's the last of all!

Trassie: You have some spatter of sense, Jack; take him away with you now.

Jack: Ah, faith, I will not take him away. 'Twould be a great aise to me to see him settled here. Sure, hasn't he my back nearly broken. Sure, aren't there hollows in my shoulders from his hands and my ribs are black and blue from the pucking he gives me. I'm a pure martyr from him.

Dinzie: Hush, Jack! Hush, pony!

Jack: Don't be calling me 'pony', Dinzie! The young lads going the road to school does be saying 'Hup!' to me now and ... (*Clicks his tongue several times*), 'Go on there, horsey!' 'Tis not fair, Dinzie.

Dinzie: Ah, sure, don't I only be coddin' you, Jack. Sure I wouldn't say a word to my own little pony. Sure, wouldn't I lick the sign of a storm.

Neelus: Wait until you hear the wind tonight!

Peadar: Awful screeching like the inside of a pig's bladder if you blew it up and left it off. The Goureen Roe was calling for the rain in the bog.

Trassie: What about the sheep?

Peadar: I counted them all near the house. They're safe enough. They know the storm is breaking. Sheep aren't as foolish as people think.

Trassie: (*Putting the coat aside – rises*) Will we have a game of cards to pass the long evening?

Peadar: 'Twould give us something to do. What games do ye play in Baltavinn?

Trassie: 'Beggar thy neighbour' or 'A hundred and ten'. I'll get the deck in the room.

(*Exit Trassie*)

Neelus: I see you with your hands around Trassie.

Peadar: I am very fond of her.

Neelus: Why are you fond of her?

Peadar: I don't know why.

Neelus: Is she fond of you?

Peadar: I hope so, Neelus. I think, maybe. She might be a little bit fond of me. I hope she is.

Neelus: (*Mournfully*) I have no one that's fond of me!

Peadar: Trassie is fond of you, man; and I'm fond of you.

Neelus: Dinzie Conlee isn't fond of me!

(Enter Trassie with a pack of cards)

Trassie: We will play 'a hundred and ten'. Neelus can deal.

(They draw chairs to the table. Neelus sits at the head, Trassie at centre and Peadar at the bottom. Neelus deals three hands of five cards each and five to the side. They examine their cards)

Neelus: We will play for pennies. I'll chance twenty.

Trassie: I pass!

Peadar: I'll pass too

(Neelus takes the five other cards quickly and examines them and throws them down again)

Trassie: 'Tis hard to beat Neelus at 'a hundred and ten'. He has a great brain for following cards.

(Neelus deals cards secondly to Trassie and Peadar, but drops the cards halfway through and sits bolt upright)

Trassie: What's wrong, Neelus?

(Neelus does not answer but sits listening. Trassie looks at Peadar)

Peadar: What's wrong, Neelus?

Neelus: It's them!

Peadar: Them! Who?

Neelus: 'Tis Dinzie and Jack, I hear Jack's feet.

Trassie: Oh, merciful God! And we having such peace.

(The three sit silently watching the door. Jack and Dinzie can be heard to approach. The door opens and Jack enters carrying Dinzie on his back)

Jack: Will I put you down, Dinzie?

Dinzie: *(Thumps Jack into back)* Aren't you in a great hurry with the poor oul' cripple. Set back a bit, let you, 'till we see what's here. Go back, pony ... back, boy ... back! *(Dinzie forces Jack to retreat while he surveys the occupants of the kitchen)* D'you see them, Jack? ... Ah, Jack, will you have a look at the faces of the craturs. Wouldn't you love to be like them? *(Loudly – pompously)* There should be no gambling allowed where there was death! 'Tis flying in the face of God. 'Tis the end of the world when people show no respect for the dead. Ye should be ashamed of yeer lives – gambling and arguing and cursing over money with yeer father roasting below in the halls of hell. Ye'll have no luck for it.

Jack: Will I put you down, Dinzie?

Dinzie: Will you go aisy! You're like an oul' woman, grumbling.

Jack: (*Wearily, first trace of anger*) Amn't I after galloping to the Wiry Glen today to see Pats Bo Bwee, and in to the town of Lenamore to Macky Flynn, the motor, and amn't I after coming here on top of it. You give me no peace or ease.

Dinzie: (*To trio*) Do you know at all what I'm going to do to Jack? I'm going to buy a pony's harness with bells on it for him and a reins made out of light leather and I'll make silver shoes for his feet.

(Dinzie gives Jack a thump in the small of the back. Jack winces and sets Dinzie down on a chair. Jack goes to the corner and begins to limber up and exercise his cramped muscles. He does this exaggeratedly. Then he takes off his coat and cap and helps Dinzie off with his. He goes through his exercises on floor)

Dinzie: (Perched on the chair) Ye'll be ready in the morning, Trassie.

(All watch him)

Trassie: Ready for what?

Dinzie: (*Vicious*) Ready to put your feet under you and leave here!

Trassie: Are you mad?

Dinzie: Not mad but in earnest! Today, myself and Jack walked all the ways to the town of Lenamore. We were telling the civic guards about Neelus and they said 'twould be safer to have him locked away.

Trassie: (*Rises*) What lies did you tell the civic guards?

Dinzie: I told what was true.

Trassie: You told lies, I know.

(*Peadar rises and glowers at Dinzie*)

Peadar: Better to take no notice of him Trassie.

(*Dinzie fumes and thumps his chair*)

Dinzie: (*Hysterically*) Listen to the lying tramp of a thatcher. Put me up on your back, Jack, 'till we kick the stomach out of him. Put me up, Jack, and we'll dance on his guts.

(*Jack goes to Dinzie's side. Peadar advances a step, fists clenched*)

Trassie: (*Command*) Peadar! (*Peadar stops*) Go out, to the stall and see if the cows are all right, and pacify the pony. He's afraid of storms.

(*Peadar looks at her doubtfully, and looks at Dinzie again, clenching his fists*)

Peadar: What about him?

Trassie: Go out now, Peadar, I'll be all right. I'll call if I want you.

(Peadar exits casting threatening looks at Jack and Dinzie)

Dinzie: That's right! Take the side of wandering villains that would murder you in your sleep.

(Dinzie scowls at Neelus. Neelus rises, looks fearfully at Dinzie, and exits)

Trassie: Why do you be always putting the heart crossways in Neelus when he has never done anything to you?

Dinzie: Because he's a blasted nuisance that should be under lock and key. We were at the Wiry Glen this morning, myself and Jack. Isn't that right, Jack?

Jack: That's right, Dinzie.

Dinzie: We were talking to Pats Bo Bwee and he's not feeling well, the poor man, after his visit to this house. He swore on his oath that Neelus will smother us all some night in our sleep. He swore on his oath that there's no madder amadán of a man from here to Donegal. Isn't that right, Jack?

Jack: He said it, all right, Trassie.

Trassie: And how much money did you give him?

Dinzie: *(Mystified)* Money! What money? Give him money for what? Explain to me, Jack, what she's saying. I never gave him money. That I might be as dead as my auntie Noney that's in her grave and my uncle Pat that was slaughtered by the turkeys in Salonika if I gave him money. Money for what?

Trassie: How much did you pay Pats Bo Bwee for saying Neelus was dangerous?

Dinzie: (*Puzzled*) What ails her, Jack, what ails her now? Sure she don't know what she's saying at all, Jack. God forgive her, she's getting wilent. 'Tis that rat's spawn of a thatcher that has this house upset. A man told me in a public house in Lenamore that you couldn't be up to the Minogues – that they were the greatest tribe of pratey-snapping mongrels from Goilldearg to the salt water.

Trassie: Go home, Dinzie. Take him home, Jack. He has no business here.

Dinzie: (*Thumps chair*) That's the respect she has for her uncle's son, her own flesh and blood, that's for her good.

Trassie: (*Firmly*) Dinzie Conlee, you're going out of this house now and you'll never come inside the door of it again. Take him up, Jack, and carry him away.

Dinzie: (*Thumps the chair, shouts*) I will not leave here! I will never leave here! My place is here! I want a little woman of my own to marry here! No one will have me if I haven't a house and land. What would you do if you had this millstone of mine on your back?

What would you do if you had only dead branches of legs? What would you do if you were never to feel the grassy ground under your feet or never to vault a gate or a ditch and you passing through land? What would you do when the fiddles are tuning up for the sets and everyone tapping toes on the stone floor? What would you do when the lads are kicking ball and you have a wild feeling to draw a kick for devilment? What would you do?

Trassie: 'Tis hard for you, I know, but it is no fault of mine. Go away from here – home!

Dinzie: (*Bitterly*) Aisy for you and for Jack here with yeer legs firm and strong and yeer straight backs. (*Shrieks*) I have nothing at all to show for myself. I have twists and turns to my body like a thorn tree. (*Roars*) I'm no fool! Dinzie Conlee's no fool. I know my value but if I have this place I will have plenty single women thinking of settling with me. (*Pleading*) Will you condemn me for that, Trassie? ... For thinking the way I do? (*Pause*) Everybody knows you yourself would have no trouble latching a man to you and I swear to God I will give you what few pounds I have to add to your fortune if you let me have this house. (*Pause*) ... And a bit o' land ... (*Pause*) ... and the few cows ... and the pony. (*Placatingly*) Won't we go visiting Neelus in his fine tall home when we get the fine day ... and the roads dry?

Trassie: (*Sincerely*) 'Tis a pity for you, but ... I have doubts about you – the way you made plans for Neelus as if he was mad.

Dinzie: (*Reverting to old, demoniacal self*) He is mad, I tell you! He's stone mad!

Trassie: How do you know but maybe 'tis yourself that's mad?

Dinzie: (*Thumps chair*) In what way would I be mad when I'm as sane as a man of ninety? Sure, you never heard anyone saying that I was mad.

Trassie: They be afraid to say it – afraid of yourself and Jack.

Dinzie: D'you hear that, Jack? Good almighty God, Jack, I say, did you hear that? I say, Jack, that's the last of all!

Trassie: You have some spatter of sense, Jack; take him away with you now.

Jack: Ah, faith, I will not take him away. 'Twould be a great aise to me to see him settled here. Sure, hasn't he my back nearly broken. Sure, aren't there hollows in my shoulders from his hands and my ribs are black and blue from the pucking he gives me. I'm a pure martyr from him.

Dinzie: Hush, Jack! Hush, pony!

Jack: Don't be calling me 'pony', Dinzie! The young lads going the road to school does be saying 'Hup!' to me now and ... (*Clicks his tongue several times*), 'Go on there, horsey!' 'Tis not fair, Dinzie.

Dinzie: Ah, sure, don't I only be coddin' you, Jack. Sure I wouldn't say a word to my own little pony. Sure, wouldn't I lick the ground under your feet, man dear, I'm so fond of you.

Jack: You have a quare way of showing it.

Dinzie: Be ready in the morning now, Trassie. Be ready with your coats and dresses and hats, and we will have the motor here in the daytime for Neelus. 'Twill be a happy day for him.

Trassie: (*In real anger*) Get out of here, you demon!

Dinzie: (*Loudly*) I won't go home! I won't! There's nothing at home for me, God help us! Nothing but an empty bed and a corner out of the way. I'll be master here, with my own woman pampering me.

Trassie: I'll bring the gun down out of the room to you.

Dinzie: Bring what you like. Nothing will move me out of this seat. My place is here!

Trassie: I will call Peadar.

Dinzie: (*Shocked*) Oooh ... Ooooooh! ... You will call Peadar! Did you ever see a paper bag blown up, full of wind. (*Puffs out his cheeks to show, then claps his hands violently*) Jack will crack in his head like that and send his brains squirting all over the ceiling. (*Draws a large clasp knife from his pocket and displays the blade*) I'll rip him open with this, the same as you'd open a sheep's belly. Bring her over to me, Jack. Bring her over and when she'll be done with me, I promise you she'll be anxious to do what I say.

Jack: Ah, Dinzie, poor oul' Trassie is only a girl. Sure she'll go all right. Say you'll go, Trassie. Tell him you'll go an' be quiet then. There's no knowing what plan he'll think of if you don't give in to him.

Trassie: I will not give in to him. Why should I? This is my place and Neelus' place and nobody, not even Dinzie Conlee, will ever put us away from what's our own.

Dinzie: (*Loudly*) Ketch her, Jack, and bring her over to me.

Jack: Ah, Dinzie, don't ask me!

Trassie: (*Nervously*) Pay no heed to him, Jack. Don't be said by him, Jack. He'll get you in jail again, and this time they won't leave you out in a hurry.

Dinzie: (*Slowly, throatily, tightening his grip upon the knife*) Ketch her, Jack, and bring her over to me, 'till I get a grip on her.

Jack: (*Afraid*) Ah, Dinzie ...

Dinzie: (*Slowly*) 'Don't mind Dinzie,' she says. 'Don't mind your own brother.' (*Hopelessly, in a wonderfully plausible vein*) O holy, holy saints, Jack, she's putting mountains between us, boy. 'Tis a terrible sight to see a person coming between two borned brothers or does she know what she's saying at all, Jack? Does she know the trouble our mother had rearing us?

Trassie: (*Determinedly*) Stop your prattle. Stop trying to work Jack's will and all our wills and clear away out of here.

Dinzie: (*Sincerely*) For the last time, Jack, I'll ask you to ketch her by the hair of the head and bring her over to where I am.

Jack: You don't mean it, Dinzie!

Dinzie: (*Fiercely*) I'll lob this knife between the breasts of her and stick her like a pig if you don't ketch her, Jack. You'll see the blade of this buried in her, and the handle standing out from her bosom like a paling stake in the depth of a hollow.

Jack: (*Turns directly towards Trassie*) I'll have to ketch you, Trassie ... (*Trassie eludes him*) Stand aisy, Trassie!

Dinzie: Blast you, you oul' fool, make a drive at her and pull her hither.

Jack: (*Confident*) I'll ketch her!

(*Jack makes another advance towards Trassie but again she eludes him and succeeds in opening the door and calling loudly*)

Trassie: Neelus! ... Neelus! (*Then quickly*) Peadar! ... Peadar!

(*As Jack advances towards the door she suddenly avoids him by*

118

availing of the table and they watch each other dartingly)

Dinzie: (*Excited*) Jump over the table at her and you have her.

(Jack outstretches both hands as if he were herding geese and tries to get Trassie into a corner)

Jack: Cush! Cush!

(Jack warily advances at one side of the table. Trassie immediately avails of the other side)

Dinzie: Pull the table out of your way and you have her.

(Jack lifts the table and drops it suddenly to face Peadar Minogue who has entered quickly, through the open door)

Dinzie: (*Yelling*) Aha, the thatcher is landed. Now Jack! Up on him, Jack! Rear up on him and we'll settle him for once and for all! (*Roar of encouragement*) Rip him, Jack. Tear Him! Stick him! Go on Jack!

(Dinzie settles back on his chair to watch the fight. Jack draws himself up to his full height and uplifts clenched fists as a fighter will. Peadar advances immediately to Trassie and surveys her worriedly)

Trassie: (*Standing nearer to Peadar*) They were trying to catch me. He wants to hunt Neelus and myself out of the house.

Peadar: (*Determinedly*) Well, they'll never do that while I'm here, Trassie.

Dinzie: Are you going to listen to Minogue the thatcher, Jack? Minogue the robber from Glashnanaon. We heard all about you, Minogue, and the thieving breeding that's in you.

Peadar: (*Menaces*) There is no bad breeding in the Minogues. Three hundred years they farmed in Glashnanaon and never a mean or cowardly act against them; never a poor man turned away from the door; never a neighbour in want of help; never a bad word thrown out against any man.

Dinzie: Your breeding is bad! Didn't you know that a foxy-haired horse-blocker from Tipperary was the first Minogue to come to Glashnanaon? Didn't you know that he gattled a loose woman under the blind eye of Glashnanaon Bridge and that's how you came by your breeding?

Peadar: It's a roaring lie! (*Anger*) It's a holy lie, you hump-backed ferret from hell. If you were a full man, I'd break every lying bone in your body.

Dinzie: (*Thumps chair with fury*) Will you listen to him, Jack? Do you hear him? Attack him! Attack him, I say! Attack and trample the life out of him. At him, Jack.

Jack: (*Assuming fighting stance*) Come on, boy!

Peadar: (*Clenches his fists and looks calmly at Jack*) I never sought after fighting but I'll fight you and beat you if that's the way of it.

Dinzie: Go on, Jack! Give him the boot!

(Jack circles menacingly around Peadar, who looks at him calmly)

Peadar: We won't fight in here. We'll fight outside in the open.

Dinzie: (*Fingering knife*) Fight him here, you coward. Fight him here!

Peadar: I'm no coward.

Dinzie: Fight him so!

Peadar: And have a knife between my shoulders when my back is turned to you? Give the knife to Trassie and I'll fight him here.

Dinzie: And have her stick Jack and maybe myself, a poor oul' cripple.

Peadar: Trassie wouldn't stick anybody.

Trassie: I'll stick him if he harms you, Peadar!

Peadar: (*To Jack*) Out here, if you're a man. (*Indicates the door*)

Jack: (*Fists up*) I'm not in dread of you boy. I'm not in dread of you.

Dinzie: (*Impatiently*) Give him one, Jack, I tell you! Draw one kick at him, into the stomach, and you'll do for him.

(Suddenly Jack draws a kick at Peadar but Peadar avoids it and walks towards the door. He turns to Jack with upraised finger)

Peadar: Out here, and I'll show you how to fight.

(Peadar exits)

Dinzie: After him, Jack. Give it to him hot and heavy, Jack boy. Put stones into your fists.

Jack: I'll bate him fair, Dinzie. He won't stand for long against Jack Conlee. I was never bested yet.

(Jack struts out)

Dinzie: Jack will tear him to ribbons with his bare hands. We'll settle for you then.

Trassie: He'll never beat Peadar Minogue. Peadar would beat two men.

Dinzie: The Conlees were never beat. If he beats Jack I'll give him this where 'twill sink. (Raises knife) I'll fool him.

Trassie: (*Advancing near Dinzie*) Would you ever think of being fair for once in your life? Have you no bit of goodness at all in you or is there nothing inside of you but evil and sin?

Dinzie: (*Violently*) Shut up! ... Shut up, I say, or I'll bury this in you.

Trassie: I'm not afraid of you! I'll warn Peadar and he'll take the knife from you. 'Tis you they'll be taking away to the home then and not Neelus. You should be in the madhouse years ago. I never in all my life saw anything as mad as you.

Dinzie: (*Erupts, and thumps chair, screams*) Shut up, I say! Shut up, or I'll dig my knife into you.

Trassie: You know 'tis the truth for me. You're a demon, a dirty sly demon and the mind is gone out of your head and there's nothing inside but sparks and flashes and frightful explo-sions and 'tis pity people should have for you and not fear.

Dinzie: (*Upraises his hands*) Stop! Stop! Stop! ... I'll kill you if you don't stop! I'll kill you for sure if you won't stop!

(*Dinzie swings the knife wildly at Trassie. He falls from the chair to the floor but comes to balance quickly and sits on the floor. Trassie flees into corner*)

(*Maliciously*) Come here to me! Come here, I say!

(*Trassie cowers in the corner. Slowly Dinzie edges nearer*)

Trassie: Keep away from me! (Calls) Peadar! Peadar! Peadar!

Dinzie: He's getting his due from Jack! No one to help you now, my doxie. No one to save you now. Come here to me. Come here, I say. (Edges closer)

Trassie: (In terror) Don't come near me! Don't come near me!

Dinzie: (*In triumph*) I'll give you something that'll put you screeching properly ... something that'll do your heart good.

Trassie: (*Cornered, looks about her hopelessly*) Oh, holy God, help me. (*Calls loudly*) Neelus! ... Neelus! ... Neelus! ... Help me, someone!

Dinzie: I'll help you when I get my hands on you!

Trassie: (*Kicks as Dinzie tries to catch her by leg*) Go away from me!

(Enter Neelus)

Trassie: Oh, thank God, Neelus. Thank God, you're here!

Neelus: (Simply, without surprise of any kind) What's Dinzie Conlee doing down on the floor, Trassie?

(Dinzie slowly turns to look at Neelus for an instant, and turns to Trassie again)

Trassie: He's trying to cut me with his knife, Neelus. Don't let him, Neelus.

Neelus: (*Advances, puzzled*) What's Peadar Minogue fighting with my cousin Jack for? You never saw such a fight, Trassie!

Trassie: (*Wearily*) Will you take the knife from Dinzie here. He has nothing in his head but killing people.

(Neelus advances and looks down at Dinzie)

Neelus: You can't kill Trassie!

Dinzie: (*Puzzled*) Kill Trassie? Who said anything about killing Trassie? A bit of sport I was having. What would make me kill my own dear cousin?

Trassie: Don't you believe him, Neelus. He's only fooling you. He wants to put you into the home, Neelus, and he wants to hunt you away from me for ever. You'll never be free again, Neelus.

Neelus: (*Puzzled*) Do you want to put me into a home, Dinzie?

Dinzie: (*Outraged*) Oh, good God almighty, them are the lies she's telling you. Sure don't you know well I wouldn't put you into a home, Neelus. I never heard such a story. Put me up on your back, Neelus. God bless you, boy bán, sure if I had my way 'tis around with a circus I'd send you every day of the week where you would be watching clowns and ponies no bigger than dogs. Put me up now on your back, Neelus.

Trassie: Don't do it, Neelus, he'll kill us all.

Dinzie: (*Coaxing*) Ah, Neelus, sure I wouldn't put a finger on one of my little cousins, if I got the use of my legs back again even. Amn't I mad about ye altogether. Yesterday week it was, I think, I said to Jack: Jack, says I, we must buy a pipe and tobacco for Neelus and train him how to smoke.

Trassie: Neelus, if you listen to him, he'll hunt you into the mad house.

Neelus: (*Looks for a long time at Trassie, then at Dinzie, then at the ceiling*) Would you promise me you wouldn't stick Trassie, Dinzie, if I put you up on my back?

Dinzie: Ah! ... I swear by all that's dead and buried belonging to me, I wouldn't do that!

Trassie: (*Hopelessly*) Oh! Don't listen to his lying tongue, my poor Neelus.

Neelus: I'll put you up so, Dinzie, if you promise.

(Neelus goes on all fours on the floor. Trassie runs out from the corner and stands with the table between herself and Dinzie. Dinzie manages to get on Neelus' back. Neelus stands holding Dinzie tightly about his neck)

Dinzie: Get a grip on me, Neelus boy. Get a grip I say and we'll have sport in plenty. 'Pon my soul and conscience but you're every bit as good as my brother Jack.

Neelus: I'll give you a good gallop.

Dinzie: A good gallop? ... Put me down, you thunderin' pothead! ... Put me down, I say!

(Suddenly Neelus twists Dinzie's hand with the knife in it and the knife falls. Dinzie struggles but his legs are dead and Neelus' grip is too strong to break with his hands)

Dinzie: Put me down, I say! (*Screeches*) Put me down! Put me down! (*Agony*) Oh, great God, take me off the back of the persecuted amadán!

Trassie: Where will you take him, Neelus?

Neelus: I'll take him for the finest gallop he ever had.

Dinzie: (*Prolonged wail*) Oooh! ... Ooooooh! ... God, take me off his back! (*Wheedling*) Put me down, Neelus, and I'll give you a lovely gold watch I have under the mattress at home. I'll give you fifty golden sovereigns I have in hiding and I'll get a handsome girl out from Lenamore to marry you if you put me down.

Neelus: (*Casual vacant*) Sure I can't, Dinzie! Sharon is waiting for me, Trassie, and Shíofra is waiting for Dinzie.

Dinzie: (*Appalled*) Shíofra ... Sharon ... He's in the power of the Devil. (*Appeals pitifully to Trassie. Screaming, struggles*) Put me down to the ground, you madman. Put me down, or I'll get Jack to kill you. Oh Lord God, put me down!

Trassie: Listen to me, Neelus! Listen to me! (Helplessly) Oh, dear God, my poor Neelus!

(Neelus goes towards door, carrying Dinzie)

Dinzie: (*High-pitched, terrified*) He's going to kill me in the lonely seas ... in the black hole ... I'll be dead ...

(*Screams*) Put me down! ... I'll kill you! ... Kill you ... Kill you ...!

(Trassie stands motionless with horror)

Oh, sweet God, he'll drown me!

Neelus: The finest gallop you ever had.

(Neelus pulls Dinzie higher on his back and exits furiously, Trassie runs to the door calling)

Trassie: (*Tearfully*) Oh, my poor foolish Neelus, come back! Come back, Neelus! (*She extends her hands*) Neelus, come back to your own Trassie ... Neelus ... Neelus ... Come back ...

(Trassie turns, her hands covering her face. Enter Peadar, hair tossed, clothes disordered, pushing a badly-beaten cowed Jack Conlee before him. Jack's face is blood-smear-ed and badly bruised. Peadar dashes him to one side, into a chair, where Jack sits, head hanging stupidly, gingerly feel-ing his wounds)

Peadar: (*As he pushes Jack aside*) There's one man bet! Where's the other fellow? Where's Dinzie?

Trassie: Oh, Peadar! ... Peadar! ... Quick! It's Neelus ... It's Neelus and Dinzie ...!

Peadar: (*Takes her hands in his*) Easy, Trassie, girl! ... Easy! ... Easy! ... Tell me what's wrong? Take control of yourself.

Trassie: Oh, Peadar ... (*Sobs*) ... Neelus ran away with Dinzie up on his back ... (Sobs) ... Hurry, Peadar! Hurry, Peadar! Go after them!

(Peadar exits. Jack rises stupidly and lurches towards the door)

Jack: The thatcher bet me but he'll never beat Dinzie. (*As he lurches out the door he passes Peadar*) You'll never beat Dinzie.

Peadar: Neelus has beaten him this time. (*Pauses, then helplessly to Trassie*) He took one mighty bound like a deer and the two of them disappeared into Sharon's grave. Poor Neelus was doing his last service to us, helping the only way he knew how.

(Trassie shakes with tears, Peadar places a hand about her shoulders)

Peadar: I will look after you, Trassie. I will stay here with you always and I'll mind you. Neelus did not know what he was doing. It was to happen the way it happened. Neelus is with his own now, with his mother and father. Don't cry now, Trassie. That is the way it was cut out for us. I'm here with you for ever, Trass ...

(Trassie looks up at Peadar tenderly. Peadar takes her hand in his. She sobs and he takes her in his arms. Enter Pats Bo Bwee agitated and excited, dressed and equipped as before)

Pats: (*Delight*) We're free! We're free at last from Dinzie Conlee. Did you see the way he took him? Did you see the way Neelus ruz like a bird with him?

(Peadar edges away a little from Trassie)

'Twas always in Neelus' head to do what he did. He has his eternal reward by now. 'Tis a great thing to be free of Dinzie Conlee.

Peadar: *(Anger)* You were as much at fault as any that Neelus is dead.

Pats: *(Palm upraised, measuring Peadar carefully)* There was no other way out of it ... *(Conciliatory)* You'll settle here and you'll be wanted here. There's fresh blood wanted in here sore.

Peadar: You're a born rogue!

Pats: Musn't we all live? What have I but the one yella cow. I couldn't be raising my hand ag'in my betters.

Peadar: Get out of here!

Pats: *(Minor warning)* Ye might want me yet.

Peadar: We'll manage well without you.

Pats: *(Head cocked aside)* Will ye though? Will ye for sure? Ye'll marry now, won't ye? Ye'll marry now and think to bring a litter o' children into the world. Ye're well-blossomed the two of ye. Maybe a little too well-blossomed for children. Ye're far advanced beyond your prime.

Peadar: We'll manage.

Trassie: (*Touches Peadar's arm*) Peadar ...

Peadar: (*Indignant*) Who's he to talk? A short while ago he was dead set against us. Anyway what counsel could he give that never had a child of his own?

Pats: (*Knowingly*) Oooh! ... Who's to tell? ... No papers to show, maybe, but they're there! (*Conspiratorially*) Ye'll want me, maybe, when ye find the days gone past with no child to keep ye awake at night.

Peadar: We'll manage.

Trassie: We're not getting younger, Peadar.

(*She links his hand. Peadar looks at her tenderly. Pats Bo Bwee seizes his chance*)

Pats: After ye're wedded, wait for news of a sickle moon in the sky. Ye must have the same soft will to ye for love. (*To Peadar*) She must have a two o' wet lips and all of a soft-ness to her. Go with her out of her warm bed at the first light of day. Let ye be fond companions in the new light. Put you something woollen around her for airly cold. Lie her down on dewy ground with the soft wool to warm her. Face her then to the first foot's fall of a flowing tide and let ye throw all thoughts of worries and woes away from ye. There must be a tide and ye must face the tide, a young silver tide with giddy antics. (*Turns to go*) And I'll be calling within the space of a year maybe to cure a blockin' of wind in a young thing or

to give advice about nursin'. (*Exiting, hand raised*)
The blessing of God attend ye. (*Exits*)

(FINAL CURTAIN)